A BARREL (

A BARREL OF STONES
in Search of Serbia

Peter Morgan

PLANET

First published
in Wales in 1997
by Planet

PO Box 44
Aberystwyth
Ceredigion
Cymru/Wales

Designed by Glyn Rees
Cover photo by Draško Gagović

Printed by Gwasg Gomer
Llandysul, Ceredigion

ISBN 0 9505188 3 2

Contents

Acknowledgements

My greatest thanks go to John Barnie and Helle Michelsen for their constant advice and encouragement. I would also like to thank several friends and colleagues for making helpful remarks about the text. Gaby Rado and Vanessa Varić gave me a few geography lessons; Branko and Branka Dimitrijević were as clued up as ever. I am also grateful for the comments offered by Celia Hawkesworth who found time in an impossible schedule to read the typescript. Sections of this book have previously appeared in *The Independent, New Statesman & Society* and *Planet.*

In Serbia itself, there were many people who did not want to be identified. For them, a round of private applause. Among others here and there, I would like to thank: Dragan Ambrozić, Shameem Bhatia, Olja Blasković, Ivan Ćolović, Vladimir Čvoro, Dessa, Professor Vojin Dimitrijević, Milena Dragićević Šesić and her colleagues at Belgrade University; Misha and Jelena, Draško Gagović and Goranka Matić at *Vreme*, Bratislav Grubaćić and the V.I.P. News Agency, Mark J. Hawker and Maja at Lomond Films, Tanja Howarth, Dr Veronika Ispanović-Radojković, Petar Janjatović, Momo Kapor, The K Foundation, Bahi at Macnet, Svetlana Kijevćanin at "Most", Perica Luković, Mihajlo Marković, Saša Marković, Mark Mazower, Mihail Milunović, Vesna and the staff at Oxfam, Belgrade, Vesna Pavlović, Milica Pesić, Zoran Petrović, Peca Popović, Slobodan Popović, Jara Ribnikar, Stanimir Ristić, Dušan Simić, Soros Foundation (Belgrade), Vlada Stakić, Branimir Johnny Štulić, Miloš Vasić, Alexander Vasović, Sian Williams, Predrag Živković and David Trethewey.

My special thanks to Dragana and Dubravka Jovanović for the twin thing — *Blizanci treba uvek da se drže zajedno* — and to family and friends.

Peter Morgan

There is nothing which so much resembles virtue as a great crime

St Just

Don't force it — use a bigger hammer

Belgrade graffiti

Introduction

It sounded simple enough to start with. Wander round a foreign country, then turn your exotic doodles into a book. That approach works well in easy going, likeable states; Serbia though is rather different. Most travel books are inspired by an attentive love for their subject. This one is driven by a more ambivalent feeling. Like many outsiders — that loud brigade of do-gooders who sweep, paramedic style, to the kerb of global disasters — I had acquired an acute suspicion of Serbia and its people. The roots of this animosity were not hard to find. Three years covering Yugoslavia's war had given me a brutal primer in the more extreme strains of Serb nationalism. It also introduced me to Croatian chauvinism: the Zagreb regime came a close second in these disaffections. But it was Serbian actions which drew my attention. Of course, it was easier to condemn Serbia from the safety of London. I wondered if my criticisms would flow as easily in a Belgrade bus queue. There were more fundamental questions too. I wanted to learn more about what had provoked the war and how it might be resolved, if at all. I might come back with my prejudices reversed — or merely refined.

Introductions are a good place to claim certain modest ambitions — and disown others. Firstly, this book is emphatically not a history of the Yugoslav conflict, 1991-1996. Several books have already covered that ground in impressive detail. "History", or at least a bloodshot version of it, has been one of the principal motors behind this war. Past events had a wilful habit of spilling into the present. On a visit to Serb-held Bosnia, I heard a press minder declare: "Don't forget — the Second World War only finished fifty years ago." That seemed to say a fair amount about the difference between his world and mine. More evidence perhaps, that watching objects through a rear view mirror really does make them appear larger than life.

The focus here is more personal. My aim was to explore how

the matter of war affected individuals; their dreams and their sense of self. To be "at war" seemed to have a double sense: it conjured a kind of location (in the same specific way as one was "at home" or "at the cinema") as well as a type of mental state. "In war, one loses all possibility of choice," wrote Slavenka Drakulić in *Balkan Express*. "There is no middle position. All of a sudden, you as Croat or Serb become responsible for what all other Croats or Serbs are doing." Yugoslavs, in her words, had been "pinned to the wall of nationhood": war had stolen their freedoms in the name of some archaic cant about national "liberation". Individuals had been whittled into "ethnic" categories. Nationality became the sole organising principle for complex societies. I wondered what happened to people when they made those choices, or had such choices forced upon them.

Secondly, this is an account of how Yugoslavia's four-year war affected Serbs, specifically those in the heartland of "Mother Serbia". This is not a trip around the front lines, at least not in the military sense. War is often seen as a form of national escape: a collective leap from a failed present into an imagined future. What were Serbs fleeing from — and where were they heading. No one seemed very sure.

There was also a kind of wishful streak to this Serbian journey. Yugoslavia's collapse had arguably been sparked in Belgrade. Given the Balkan habit of dispatching politicians in wooden boxes rather than ballot boxes, I figured it would end there too. Although Serbia itself was far from the battlegrounds of Vukovar or Sarajevo, war infected every aspect of life. Loyal Serbs will not enjoy the parallel, but I imagined Nineties Belgrade to be rather like Berlin in the Forties, "a lost city at the bottom of the sea." Here again, the world had been turned upside down by a kind of mass psychosis. I wondered how Serbs had reached that warped state and equally important, how they would recover from it.

The initial idea for this journey came in the spring of 1995, as Bosnia's war went into its fourth year. By then, Yugoslavia had become a byword for primal brutality: Sarajevo had taken Beirut's unloved place as a symbol of hell on earth, an adjective in itself. International efforts to stop the war were ineffective. One weary diplomat described Europe's Bosnia policy as "drawing a circle around the country and then watching it burn." Which was all very well, except outsiders got scorched as well. United Nations troops formed a Protection Force which plainly failed to protect: when the Bosnian Serbs overran the so-called "safe areas" of Srebrenica and Žepa in July 1995, the UN mission was fatally eroded.

Two startling moves in the summer of that year turned the Balkan equation on its head. First, a newly rearmed and retrained Croatian Army (with a little help from the US cavalry) retook the Serbian region of Krajina, forcing tens of thousands of Serbs to flee. Croatia's new military force moved on to Bosnia, where Radovan Karadžić's ragged Serb army chose to cut and run.

The second surprise came in September. Somewhat late in the day (and that was surely part of their calculations), NATO planes battered Bosnian Serb positions with bombs and video cameras. Just over two months later, Serbia's President Milošević signed the Dayton peace agreement. This committed Bosnia's Serbs to hand a third of their land over to the Bosnian/Croat Federation. 51 per cent of the country would be controlled by this Federation, 49 per cent by the Serbs. Bosnia would become a mongrel space: a "Republic" with two opposing heads on the same body. Few believe that Bosnia-Hercegovina will ever exist again in its Yugoslav form. In the clamour of peace, few raised the most painful question either. If Yugoslavia's conflict could be stopped in its tracks so quickly, then why hadn't this option been taken in 1991, before Bosnia was turned into a vast cemetery? At the time of writing, the republic was not at war, but neither was it at peace.

In Serbia, there was a more rueful spirit. A wartime phrase from Germany came to mind: "Enjoy the war while you can, because the peace will be terrible." My first reaction to Balkan life was to set my watch back rather than forward: Central European Time meant returning to a historical no-man's land midway between

World War One and World War Two. This was the realm of *Duck Soup* and Neutralia, Evelyn Waugh's dim Central European state.

More frequent visits made me change that view. Far from being a throwback to Europe's "tribal" past as many commentators claimed, Yugoslavia was a glimpse into one possible future. By ridiculing this phenomenon, I was somehow denying its danger. Despotism, Serbian style, used highly modern instruments: television being the most obvious example. Anyone who believes a mass media "global village" will reduce the risk of civil warfare has clearly never watched TV Serbia, or any of the private TV stations which clog its unlicensed airwaves. There's more than enough poison — and history — to go around.

At times, there was a kind of fictive quality to these experiences which I wanted to capture. To say that it felt "like a movie" would be rather too glib, but there was a sense in which everything was out of scale, both physically and morally. Rolling up to a Bosnian checkpoint to face a doped-up teen with a Kalashnikov was hard enough to take in; bumping into the alleged war criminal Arkan in the lobby of a Belgrade hotel was memorably unpleasant. Now there are some tough ethical questions to face in situations like that. One can hide (as most of the quivery bellboys did), or attempt a citizen's arrest on behalf of the War Crimes Tribunal. People win medals for things like that. I took the third option and scurried back to my double-bolted room.

I'm glad to say my childish fear of driving had one real benefit during these excursions. By being forced to travel on Serbia's dreadful buses, I met plenty of normal people and a fair batch of odd ones (the slightly deaf aromatherapist from Loznica sticks in my mind). Long journeys encouraged bad jokes and rambling stories. Some of them sounded too tall to be true, so naturally I've included them here. Off guard, people expressed the kind of thoughts which will keep the past alive for at least one more generation.

What follows is an account of my wanderings around Serbia in the autumn of 1995. The first few chapters explore Serbian nationalism in its various forms. The focus then turns to those who have opted out of this war society. Despite impressions to the contrary, Serbia is a multi-ethnic country: in a pre-war census only 64 per cent of the population described themselves as Serb. One could argue that many of Serbia's problems are rooted in this national contradiction.

The next section returns to a conflict at the heart of this book: the complex relationship between Orthodox Serbs and Muslims, as expressed through the struggle for Srebrenica. The final chapters take the Yugoslav drama to its temporary resolution at the Peace Signing in Paris. Throughout these episodes, I have tried to show how people saw these events; how they *interpreted* them. Nations are first imagined in the mind: I wanted to examine the visions which had lodged there.

To begin with, I was unable to understand Serbia's emotive signs and intricate obsessions. There were prejudices within prejudices, grievances laid upon outrages. In time, some patterns began to emerge and brought the country into clearer relief. I hope it goes some way towards pleasing one Belgrade friend, who likened foreign correspondents to clumsy drama critics. "You always fumble into the theatre half way through the second act, make a lot of noise and then try and review a play you've hardly seen." What's more, he complained, we always blocked the audience's view. A fair point. After all, we are often working in other people's darkness.

1 Srebrenica

Zoran arrived early in the afternoon, when the attack was almost over. His first shot showed a country lane edged with summer green. Sunlight fanned through the dense branches. Without warning, a tourist bus hurtled into frame. Judging from the vehicle's alarming tilt, its driver was in a hurry. Before the brown mist could subside, two more coaches scuttled across the picture. Their windows were empty. Panning left, the camera caught a soldier idling along the roadside, a rifle strapped to his shoulder.

Zoran's second image came from the dark interior of a moving car. An old tank hogged this picture, framed by the fly-swabbed windscreen. After a few seconds of grunting tank, the camera shifted to the left. A factory compound passed behind a screen of barbed wire. "Is that the UN base?" someone shouted. Another voice added its approval. On the roof of the UN compound, there was a sky blue sign with the word DUTCHBAT rendered in white capital letters. To the right, a row of buses were parked in the sun. We were going somewhere with these tanks and coaches: we were going to relieve and punish.

The next picture went by so fast I had to stop the video machine and replay the tape. Slowly again, I saw a group of country women, their heads shying under patterned scarves as if expecting blows. Some walked; others had broken into a controlled run. Among the Muslim wives and mothers, the impatient lens picked out a young girl with a baby couched in her white arms. An evacuation was taking place, the women compelled by a force behind the viewfinder.

From the file of women, our view switched to a row of men walking in the shadow of parked coaches. Most of them were old, white haired and smartly jacketed, a lumpy bundle of clothes under each arm. For some reason, there were only husbands and fathers in this group. A young soldier, whom I took to be a Serb, was ordering them about. "Left!" he shouted. "Keep on the left!"

One captive stared directly into the lens. His terrified eyes caught mine and I looked away, ashamed. Zoran's camera lingered, gathering banal details of the event. Above, there was the indifferent sun. Beneath, walkie-talkies sang and motors revved: normal devices at the service of the abnormal. Two elderly men passed in front of me. One wore a brown hunting cap, the other, a black beret. Both of their faces were riven by feeling, by a sense stronger than fear. As the two prisoners shuffled away, their eyes strayed to the right. With a brief twist of focus, Zoran's camera followed their desperate gaze. His wide shot revealed the shameful whole: a row of women walking down one side of the coach, the men on the other.

I stopped the tape. Viewing these pictures was a discomforting experience. They demanded a response which I was unable to give, isolated by time and distance. Of course, I could pretend. Television production has a kind of cheap sorcery: one can rewind pictures and examine them a hundred times if necessary. People on tape were routinely spun back in time and then rudely rushed forward. My reluctance on this occasion was, I supposed, a form of respect. I knew the men in this film — the elderly pair, the man pleading with the hidden viewer — were probably no longer alive. I had been watching their last moments. They were part of Srebrenica's dead.

Zoran Petrović's film came to our office via a Dutch intermediary. The word was that Petrović had become angry at the way his film was being shown for free around the world. Now he wanted some financial credit. Petrović was a freelance cameraman from Belgrade. He had arrived in Srebrenica on the afternoon of Thursday July 13th, as Bosnian Serb troops completed their attack on the former United Nations safe area. His film contained sights which lodged in my heart and refused to leave. Petrović had used a small Video 8 recorder rather than a professional camera: his pictures were often out of focus or slightly shaky, yet they had an immediacy which made me flinch from the screen.

There was another aspect to this unease. As a conceited by-product of my job, I had come to regard cameras — rather naively — as forces for good: an accountable eye on events. Yet in Srebrenica the world had proceeded as if the camera was not there, as if it did not matter. We craved "realism", but what could one do with reality?

My mental balance had been upset by the pitiless lens. Somehow, the format did not seem appropriate either. In affluent societies, video cameras had become the favoured way to record group events. Like still photography, they created and preserved images of happiness: a rowdy wedding, the Spanish holiday, a baby's first canter. On this occasion, the camera was being used to record what the United Nations War Crimes Tribunal later called "scenes from hell, written on the darkest pages of human history." Now and then, a digital display would flick on to the screen, giving mundane details of time and date. I started to note timings: a way to account for pain. Thus: 13.07.95, 16.48.00: the chink of bullet casings rolling down a hot road, a round of rifle snaps in the forest. And I wondered what kind of images other holiday cameras were recording at this time, on this date.

There was a larger shame, if that was possible. A crime had taken place and nothing had been done. Men, women and children — Muslims from Srebrenica and its outlying villages — were rounded up outside a United Nations base. Many of these men had died. Later, the UN said that up to 8000 had disappeared: the population of a small town. I knew how this episode would end, and it was not a good ending. Reluctantly, I went back to the tape and completed the story. Events happened quickly. Buses reappeared, their speeding windows filled with tearful mothers and children. Serb tanks shuttled up narrow roads, leaving heavy tracks on the melted surface. Every time a group of Serb soldiers confronted the camera, they raised their thumb, index and third finger in a national salute. Of the Muslim men there was no sign, save for their clothing. At the rim of every shot lay piles of abandoned garments: bundles and bags left like rubbish sacks at the gates of the United Nations base; cardigans and jumpers stretched out on the sun-bleached grass.

The Muslim men had fled. Thousands had escaped into the woods around Srebrenica to evade the Bosnian Serb Army. They were captured in small groups. Late that afternoon, Zoran's camera caught up with one Serb patrol and their Muslim prisoners. They were in a wide clearing where the grass reached knee height and a falling sun left its shadow. Another file of men tramped towards the lens. This time, they were a lot younger, dressed in short-sleeved shirts and jeans. ("They've taken their uniforms off and left them up in the woods," said one Serb soldier, "so they can come down in civilian clothes".) A tall, balding man approached the camera. He was wearing a pale blue shirt, half buttoned up. The skin on his face was stretched to its human limit. The compressed lips and rigid eyes imparted a sense of acute fear. No explanation was needed: he knew that death was near and was summoning the will to face it. The man walked up to Zoran.

"Where have you been?" asked the cameraman.

"I don't know it myself," said the man. His voice was soft and hesitant. "From a desert of a sort."

"How long have you been there?"

"Two days and two nights"

"Where are your guns?"

"I didn't have a gun," the man whispered. "I am a civilian."

While Zoran talked with the condemned man, other prisoners passed in mute groups. There were rifle shots nearby.

"Were you frightened?" asked Zoran.

The man shook his head, unable perhaps to accept the stupidity of this question.

"Of course I was frightened," he said. Before he could continue, there was a derisive laugh from behind the camera: the jeer of a Serb soldier standing next to Zoran.

"Oh come on, old man," said the voice. "Don't be scared. Fuck you! What are you scared of! Let's go."

The prisoner's petrified face suggested this was exactly why he was scared. He gave the camera a final nod and then walked off. Turning away, the back of his shirt came into view: a blue canvas blotted with recent blood.

Faced with such brutal scenes, the observer struggles for a proper definition; a handhold for the mind. I could not find one. Within days of these pictures being taken, it was clear that Srebrenica had seen the largest single massacre of the Bosnian war. Zoran's camera had recorded the early stages. The exact circumstances of these deaths were disputed, yet there were reports of mass graves, of bodies heaped along forest paths. Some of these deaths could be presented as casualties of war, but the scale of killing suggested a deeper pathological motive.

After the killings, there were routine searches for meaning. A familiar theme emerged from the immediate newsprint. Srebrenica's Muslims, the media explained, were victims of an extreme Serb nationalism, a neo-fascist mentality which combined ethnic exclusivism and organised violence. Such ideas had been used throughout Bosnia's war, the press reminded us, to justify "ethnic cleansing": the forced expulsion of Muslims from their homes across the Republic. All sides in Bosnia's complex war had used this tactic at some time or another. Serb forces though had taken the technique to its extreme.

Most of this I knew and understood. Yet there was a marked imaginative gap between what I had *seen* and what I had read. Zoran Petrović's material seemed to show the first phases of a planned massacre. But to the media, the killings were beyond comprehension, another of Bosnia's appalling incidents and therefore almost impossible to explain. Perhaps four years of Balkan war had made reason redundant. At the same time, the only way to understand this mass murder was to chart the malign dreams and deeds which made it permissible. I remembered that invisible Serb soldier who had laughed at the "old man" in the clearing, at the thoughts which filled his victorious head. Explanations were hidden there, if anywhere. As for the source of these angry visions, they were to be found in Serbia proper. My visit there had acquired an unwanted definition. I wanted to know why Srebrenica had been allowed to happen. There was plenty of evidence for the prosecution, but I also wanted to hear what Serbs would say in their own defence. To make sense of this question, one had to try and make sense of Serbia.

If Srebrenica was a crime, then what kind of crime had been committed? Genocide is described in the *Oxford English Dictionary* as "the deliberate extermination of a people or nation." The organised killing of thousands of Muslim men appeared to come within that definition. Historian Irving Horowitz offered a more specific set of criteria. Genocide, he wrote, was "a structural and systematic destruction of innocent people by a state bureaucratic apparatus." Both formulas addressed the mechanics of mass killing, but did not explore their fundamental motives. One could argue that for such enormous crimes, no motive can be remotely adequate. Yet within the duty of remembering, there lies an obligation to explain.

In *The Rise and Fall of the Third Chimpanzee*, the American physiologist Jared Diamond distinguishes between four overlapping types of mass murder. First, genocide can be triggered by a struggle for land between two unequal parties: the stronger group overwhelms the weaker in order to suppress resistance. In the second category, genocide is the violent solution to a civil power struggle. Such conflicts usually involve two groups with mutually conflicting claims to land, wealth and political authority. One group seeks a decisive end to this confrontation by exterminating the other. Both definitions, Diamond claims, have a common dynamic: the victims are seen as significant obstacles to the killers' claim on land and power. Diamond's third category involves what he calls "scapegoat killings": genocidal acts in which weak minorities are blamed for national failure. Finally, he finds genocidal urges in the extremities of racial or religious persecution.

Yugoslavia provided relevant examples of all these categories, along with a haze of complications. Serbs seeking to legitimise their own actions had drawn on the traumatic reserves of history. Orthodox Serbs had been victims themselves. Under the Ottoman Empire, Serbs had been subjected to centuries of Muslim rule.

During the Second World War, tens of thousands of Serbs had lost their lives at the hands of Croatia's pro-Nazi regime. In the eyes of Serbian apologists, past atrocities were a sufficient defence. Outsiders, myself included, were unconvinced. Blaming the past looked like a convenient way to elude the present. The Serbian defence did however raise one related point, an issue which needed to be clarified. Searching for a distinction between mass murder and genocide, Jared Diamond highlights the role of intent. In some cases, he points out, killings are inspired in "retaliation" for past deaths, the drastic response to a series of murders and counter murders. The main question, in Diamond's view, is at what point retaliation becomes organised killing, or genocide. One needs to find the point where reason runs out.

I was looking for answers to these general questions. I also had some more specific queries about Zoran Petrović's video. Second time around, his visual account created doubts in my mind. Zoran's film claimed to present a "true" impression of what had happened in Srebrenica. Yet it was not giving us the whole picture. At several points I noticed the images of round ups and deportations were interrupted by pieces of blank tape. The original material had been replaced by a black screen, which meant Zoran had rolled with the lens cap screwed on. Sometimes this happens by accident: a loose finger on the flighty controls, and there goes a morning's work. This time, the deletions had been done on purpose. Sections of Zoran's film had clearly been erased later when he returned to Belgrade. Whenever Zoran filmed his lens cap, the camera microphone had dutifully picked up a new soundtrack. The results were bizarre and somewhat grotesque: in one deleted part, the black tape was accompanied by sounds of a child playing with a pop gun.

Zoran's self-censorship raised a number of points. As a photo-journalist — and a Serb — he had evidently found most of that day's events quite acceptable to film. There was no sense of recoil or dismay. But what exactly had he taken out? One incident in particular had stayed in my mind. About half way through the tape (Time Code: 13.07.95, 16.12.05), the camera chanced on a couple of Serb soldiers lying in the shade. They were both youngish — late teens, gap toothed — with an air of rangy violence. The taller one was wreathed in bandoleers, weighed down with bullets. An informed viewer might have put these characters in a special unit: an execution squad perhaps. The bandoleered one had a pistol tied at his neck with a piece of white string like a referee's whistle. As the camera zoomed, he picked up a pistol and unloaded its magazine. After a brief check, the cartridge was returned to its casing. The soldier's wrist was sealed in an orange glove: protection, I guessed, for his killing hand. With a swift flick of the wrist, the soldier turned his pistol towards the grass and made a trial shot, a rehearsal of murder.

This was hard to watch. As the soldiers grinned, Zoran's camera pulled out and around, round towards a clearing on the left. I slowed the tape down to half speed. There were about thirty men in the sunlight, surrounded by Serb guards. Muslim men with T-shirts or with bare tops: more captives from the hillsides. The camera rested long enough for me to make a fatal connection between the bandoleers and the clearing. Then, a picture shudder and black. Zoran had erased the rest of the incident from his tape. Something had happened, something which Zoran did not want to remember. Maybe there was one event which even the camera had been ashamed to witness.

2   A Serbian Phrase Book

Somewhere over Hungary, the captain decided it was time to introduce himself. After some extended throat clearing, he welcomed us on board and promised a landing in about half an hour. His voice was furry and tired: a sixty-a-day man, I guessed. I had been expecting a bit more chat: the usual airborne patter about wind speeds and cruising altitudes, but that was that. After two hours in Economy, I was becoming a firm fan of Yugoslav Airlines and their restrained hospitality. Fly with most other airlines and there's hardly a minute to yourself: lunch buckets and roasted towels land in your lap, cabin staff confuse help with harassment. There was no such trouble with Yugoslav Airlines: the blue draped stewardesses respected our privacy, and expected us to respect theirs. Apart from an emergency rations dinner about one hour in, I was left alone over Europe for the entire flight.

Plane journeys are a kind of cultural air-lock: a swift staging post between home and abroad. They're also the point at which one starts to get fruitfully lost. London's crocheted avenues fell away in autumn shade, an abandoned plan. Bored, I started to imagine shapes on the pillowy clouds. When sky sketching lost its charm, there was always the in-flight movie: an antique trip through Yugoslavia's national parks, set to the patriotic sounds of Richard Clayderman. Time passed. When we broke through the clouds once more it was early evening, a spine of amber lights beneath us.

After the usual thump and jiggle of landing, our captain came on again — which was considerate — and told us this was Belgrade, just in case anyone thought we'd bowled up in Wichita or Newcastle. I took one step inside the terminal and it all came back.

Before I left home, Sanja from Sarajevo told the following joke. At some time in the future, she says, Yugoslavia sends a rocket into space. (She pauses: "No, that's not the joke.")

Anyway, on board there are two Serbs, one Croat and one Bosnian. After a few days spinning around in orbit, they land on the moon. "What beautiful scenery!" cries the Croatian astronaut as he steps on to the lunar surface. "It's just like our Dinaric mountains: this must be Croatian land!" The Bosnian astronaut is equally excited. "One can only find such wonderful sights in my homeland," he sighs. "Surely, we are in Bosnia." The two Serbs are completely silent. After a while, one of them takes out a pistol and shoots his fellow Serb in the head, while reciting a nationalist proverb. "Wherever there is a Serbian grave," the killer intones, "that is Serbian land."

I retold the gag to some London friends, who didn't get it at all. "Is that meant to be a joke?" *one of them said, frowning. Somehow he thought it wasn't right to make fun of wars like that. Another friend just felt it was sad: perhaps the moon was the only innocent place now, she said. And by the way, what was the punchline?*

Dragan had brought his four-wheel-drive to the airport: a red Jeep-type vehicle which he used to take TV crews around Bosnia. These backyard safaris netted good money: so good that Dragan and his wife had recently flown to Florida for a week to visit their bank accounts. We had not met for over a year. He looked much the same: thin and hangdog, though now some white streaks poked out from under his black baseball cap.

Along the dusky slip road there were faded billboards for alien goodies like Marlboro and Coke. Serbia in October was warmer than I expected: the truck's open windows let in dense, chemical air.

"Everyone drives here," said Dragan. "It's just like America."

"How was Florida?"

"Good."

"And coming back?"

Dragan sighed. He spoke a kind of downtown English: familiar words turned in a flat American accent.

"Well I didn't feel at home there," he said. "But then I don't feel at home here either."

We joined a deserted motorway, heading for Belgrade. This was the renowned Highway of Brotherhood and Unity. The first distinct images I could remember from the Yugoslav war were taken somewhere along this road. In July 1991, a shimmering file of JNA tanks shuffled down the *Autoput* towards Croatia and Slovenia; women and children cheered from every bridge as if watching a carnival. We all stood and watched with them: it was an internal affair, we said.

"The only place we feel really comfortable, really ourselves is in our home," Dragan went on. "That's the only place we don't feel strange. Outside has changed, Belgrade has changed. It's not my city anymore."

"What's changed?"

"The people. It really hit me when we came back from Florida. We got to Amsterdam and waited for a connecting flight to Belgrade. We sat there with lots of other Serbs and they were just like little kids!

"They were so glad to get on the plane, all these Serbs who'd been travelling the world. The men loosened their ties and started to drink. Women walked up and down the aisles smoking while the plane was taking off, that kind of thing. They didn't care anymore. They were back on home ground, they could do what they wanted."

War seemed to have encouraged this wilful streak. Without the discipline of peace, people felt excused from behaving sensibly. Living under the shade of immense crimes, small offences went unchecked, unnoticed.

Dragan talked about home. They had bought an Alsatian. "My wife says he's a real Serb dog," said Dragan. "He's very proud, and always getting into fights." If the dog didn't scare people off, he added, there was always a revolver under the sofa.

Belgrade started in a slur of grey apartment blocks. We passed some roadside bar, a single lamp beckoning from a shuttered doorway. The drabness was generic Communist: bus shelters built like steel umbrellas, the usual stuttering cars. The city was already closing in, imposing its war fever. On the left there was a long strip of corrugated metal, coated with posters from Serbia's last Presidential election. The thuggish face of nationalist Vojislav Šešelj stared out at the traffic. Ahead, one of the city's more bizarre landmarks rushed up. The Yugotours tower had a large digital display on its roof which doled out standard information about date, time and temperature. It looked like a king-sized clock radio: the futuristic allusions made it appear painfully dated.

"Were you homesick in Florida?" I asked Dragan.

"No," he said. "Only dog sick."

Five facts about the former Yugoslavia, courtesy of Yugoslavia — Republics and Provinces *(London, 1980).*

1. The Federal Republic of Yugoslavia (b. 1945 — d. 1991) occupied 2.56 per cent of the total land area of Europe. Serbia made up around 30 per cent of Yugoslavia.

2. "Since the War, the newly constituted Republic of Yugoslavia has moved ahead with giant strides."

3. "In 1945, Bosnia-Hercegovina had a total of 30 kilometres of asphalt roads, as against 5,000 kilometres today."

4. The medieval bridge of Mostar was widely celebrated. One writer compared the Bosnian monument to a shiny rainbow turned to stone. Another likened it to a crescent moon, drawn down from the sky. The bridge was destroyed by Croatian shells in 1993.

5. In Ottoman times, Belgrade was known as "The House of Wars".

The next day I sat in the hotel room and made a lot of phone calls. I left my name at Institutes and Ministries, Faculties and Corporations. The voices were polite but wary: if I called back in three days time they said, someone would be able to help. I gave them my number just in case. This was the way it was supposed to work: throw a few lines into the pond and hope someone takes the bait. Except this was Serbia and no one really wanted to discuss the war, or the future. Back in the late Eighties, when Slobodan Milošević launched his national programme, Serbs couldn't stop talking about Serbia. There was a sense of excitement: the sort of suppressed thrill people get when breaking the rules. Serbs were reminded of their supposed historic right to live in one state. Such talk had been taboo under Tito for obvious reasons. Yet prohibition did not kill nationalism: it merely drove the product underground, elevating its untested value.

Nationalism elbowed in with childish promises — Serbia would be as wealthy as Sweden, a peaceful nation — and people voted for it. "Even the deaf hear the voice of the nation!" insisted one contemporary banner.

The most worrying thing about Serbia in 1995 was that people were still voting for national salvation, despite all evidence to the contrary. Serbia was not as wealthy as Sweden (though it had some Swedish wealth, thanks to the Scandinavian soldiers who came here with the UN and NATO). Nor was it a nation at peace with itself: police work was the only growth industry. In Western Europe, inflation rates of 2 per cent a year put voters in a tantrum. In Serbia, people endured inflation at two per cent a minute in the winter of 1993 and then returned the Socialists to power.

There had been marches; there had been street protests; Milošević should have been overthrown and replaced with a more tolerant leader. At least that was what visitors like me thought as we toured Serbia in our air conditioned minibuses. If we had looked and listened a little closer during that campaign in December 1993, we might have learnt something.

Like the fact that Serbian society remained, at its core, deeply traditional. The political "class" was small, and mainly based in the larger towns and cities. That term covered both politically active people (elected officers and party members) and the politically alert (those who habitually read above, below and between the lines). And small meant small: one academic numbered this political class at around ten thousand, from a population of ten million. Add an estimated illiteracy rate of thirty per cent, and one didn't have the ingredients for a vivid or self-aware political scene.

Most Serbs still regarded civil politics as a burden rather than a privilege. Choice bewildered people. Cynics cherished the story of the peasant from southern Serbia who told Opposition leader Vuk Drašković that he would gladly vote for him — if he was already President. In rough times, this respect for authority hardened into blank allegiance. Sanctions were supposed to bring Serbia to heel: instead, they drove people closer to the regime and confirmed their historical self-image as persecuted outsiders. Everyone used the same phrase to describe the UN penalties: they were unjust and unwarranted sanctions. Sometimes it came out like one portmanteau word, angrily parroted. The harder one struck the Serbian nail, the further it sunk into the wood.

Serbia's governing clique must have loved it. Having done everything wrong, they could do nothing wrong. By the early months of 1995, their remarks were sounding deliberately sarcastic, as if goading their people to respond. Zoran Lilić, a former male model turned Milošević crony told Hungarian Radio that "in the former Yugoslavia, we had Greater Serbia and Greater Croatia, because all the Serbs and the Croats lived in one state." Four years of war and more than two hundred thousand people dead or missing, according to the United Nations, and a friend of Mr Milošević says that, on balance, the old system was pretty good.

I sat on my hotel bed and stared at the city across the Sava. Rusted tugs and steamers lined the river banks, moored like bathtime toys. The Sava churned blankly. Few boats passed through this river stretch any more: the unjust and unwarranted sanctions had seen to that. Belgrade had shut down: this town was closed for business.

I remembered days like this from previous visits: days when nothing in particular happened, full stop. Something strange had happened to time here, but I couldn't yet work out what. Everything seemed physically normal — glum piles of brick and cement, folk of regular height and girth — yet events didn't unfurl in the way one expected. They seemed to stall in sluggish circles, revolving around the same people and the same mistakes. The future had been suspended: there was only the present and the past. Time congealed at certain fixed points, lives failed to progress. In my notebook was a remark by one Belgrade art critic, Branislav Dimitrijević: "If there is no progress," he wrote, "does it matter how quickly it will not appear?"

Petar returned my call. He couldn't help with the time question, but he had some ideas about Srebrenica. He wanted to talk about a mentality, a frame of mind.

"If you want to understand Serbs," he said, "there are only three words you need to know: *Inat, Javašluk* and *Sevdah*."

Petar was a big rock and roll fan: Clapton, The Who, The Rolling Stones. He had seen them all, before all of this. Petar's beard was chalk white, though he still wore the rocker's uniform: denim jacket, jeans and a T-shirt listing dates for *The Scorpions — European Tour*.

"There's no real, direct translation for *Inat*," he mumbled. "Maybe you'd say it's when your heart overrules your head. *Inat* describes those occasions when you do what you want, even though you've been told it's bad for you. You know this thing will cause you harm, but you do it anyway because it's your choice."

One didn't have to look far to find this side of the Serbian character. The Bosnian Serbs had arguably run their entire foreign policy on the *Inat* principle: the siege of Sarajevo, the seizure of Srebrenica and Žepa, the capture of UN soldiers. Radovan Karadžić seemed to enjoy the attention. To start with, *Inat* bought a dividend for the Bosnian Serbs. Mediators and media tourists scampered to their door; there was even an occasional jaunt to Geneva or London under the guise of "peace talks". After Srebrenica, NATO bombing raids finally undercut the *Inat* myth, though even defeat became a source of pride. Serbs were so tough, people said, that they only gave in after being flattened by NATO — that was *Inat* for you.

Heart over head, fight rather than flight: *Inat* was a mental

reflex from the long days of Turkish occupation, from the struggle for Serbian autonomy in the nineteenth century. Outsiders —
especially bossy outsiders — still roused Serbian suspicions and
drove them to erratic displays of independence.

One petulant example came to mind. I heard about a Bosnian
Serb who had walked into a toy shop in Germany and seen a pack
of playing cards by the counter. In bad German, he asked for the
price of the cards. The shopkeeper frowned at his scruffy Serb
customer. "They're far too expensive for you," he said. Now the
Serb didn't want to buy the cards, but once he heard the German
shopkeeper say they were too dear for him, he lost his temper. "I
didn't ask if they were too expensive," he shouted. "Just tell me
the price!" The shopkeeper gave him the price and the Serb
bought his precious cards. "And do you know," he said proudly,
"I took them home and didn't know what to do with them. I've
never played cards in my life."

The second word in Petar's Serbian Phrase Book was *Javašluk*.
I liked the way it spilled off the tongue: Yah-Vah-Shlook, a
rambling, shaggy vocable, like something one would say after a
messy sneeze.

Again, there was no comparable word in English — these were
local moods rather than common codes — although Petar did
make an attempt.

"Basically, *Javašluk* means you don't give a shit," he said. "It's
lazy behaviour, irresponsible conduct: the kind of thingwhich
sometimes leads to damage or injury."

Javašluk was a tendency to shoddiness. Petar thought of an
example straight away.

"Last week I took my car to the garage to get something fixed,"
he said. "When I picked it up, that fault had been sorted out, but
there were two new problems with the car. I complained to the
mechanic, but he just shrugged his shoulders. That's *Javašluk*."

I'd experienced *Javašluk* in a more mundane form. Hunger —
and the wish for a simple, five minute meal — had driven me and
a friend to McDonalds (Mek-Donalds to Serb purists) on the
city's busy Terazije. All the usual options (Big Mek, Mek with
Cheese) were splayed across a plastic board, all except French

fries. The chips were off, my friend explained, because Yugo-slavs couldn't make them. They didn't have the machines for it. Before the war chips were bussed in from Turkey, then that traffic had stopped because of sanctions. My friend wriggled her shoulders in defeat, the standard *Javašluk* gesture. Petar understood. *Javašluk* was a discreet form of political control.

"The worst thing about all this," he said, "is how it eats up your time. Once you've got the car fixed, bought food and repaired the gas heater in the apartment, there's no time left for anything else. No time for life means no time to dream."

Petar's fatalism turned out to be a pretty fair definition of the third word in his lexicon. *Sevdah* described a strain of deep melancholy, the sort of self-destructive sadness often celebrated in morose ballads.

"*Sevdah* means people get thoroughly pissed," he said. Nothing terribly unusual about that, I thought. But Petar insisted Balkan drinking jags were unique in their rigour. My memories of *Sevdah* centred on one all night drinking den called *Kula* (Tower) in the Zemun district of the city. *Kula* was a converted church with a couple of bars stuffed into the belfry. Most nights, the ground floor bar was given over to a Gypsy band from Northern Serbia. Now and then, the group would stroll off for a breather and we'd be left with some taped folk music. These jittery tunes had an unvarnished *Sevdah*-like quality about them: *I'm pasting up the wallpaper with my tears* usually hit the spot. But the loudest cheer went up for the family favourite: *I can't wait for the Mother in Law to die / So we can take over the apartment.*

Sevdah then was what you felt when your faith in *Inat* ran out. It evoked a bleaker, nihilistic mood. The three words provided a neat sketch of the Serbian character: all of them helped to explain the momentum of war. I also liked the fact they were impossible to translate: somehow that made them even more authentic. Even within a world culture, I thought, there were still some ideas and actions which remained part of national lives. I told Petar. He nodded.

"A nice theory," he said. "A pity that they're all based on

Turkish words."

Petar scratched his beard and we talked about rock and roll.

Milan would not let me use his real name. He taught economics "at a Serbian university" and did not want his opinions attached to his name. I asked Milan for an example of *Inat* and he laughed.

"The greatest example of *Inat*," he said, "is my decision to stay here."

He was a short, smartly dressed man with a trim beard. English words flew out in a high pitched chatter, sprinkled with ums and ahs. One has to be a certain age (or mentality) to catch this allusion, but to me he sounded like Professor Yaffle, the wooden bird cum bookend who hung out with *Bagpuss*. We talked in his office, a white walled box with no apparent heating.

"*Inat* is a kind of negative pride," he went on. "Maybe it was a way to console Serbs when they were under occupation, a way to preserve their identity."

"Like a form of protection?"

"Exactly. *Inat* helped explain events as well — disasters, deaths, that kind of thing."

I wondered what he made of the Serbian economy. Yugoslavian industry had been in a poor state before 1991: war drove each warring republic into bankruptcy. Serbia's leaders had plundered banks and factories to finance a war in Croatia and then in Bosnia. As a result, the economy was already badly damaged before sanctions were imposed. The trade embargo reinforced that dereliction.

Milan shook his head.

"All they can do is put paint on dirty walls," he said. "The basic problem is they're all communists with that State way of thinking — even in Slovenia! (the former Yugoslav Republic which broke away in 1991). Look at the Slovenes: the same walls except the coating is a little better. In Slovenia, they use wallpaper."

"And the future?"

"Well, there will have to be a third Yugoslavia in some form." Milan was grinning now, as if anticipating this huge black joke.

"You know, we've got all the right conditions for it. A common language, a common culture, even mixed families."

"How would it work?" I asked, incredulous.

"Oh, you know. A kind of Benelux sort of thing."

"And what would they call it ?"

"Not Yugoslavia, that's for sure. But we've tried different names before. After Tito's death, we even thought of changing the country's name then."

"What was the new name going to be?"

"Titanic." Milan pronounced the word Tee-tan-ic to rhyme with Tito. After a brief snigger he repeated the word, in case I hadn't got the joke. Or maybe he just enjoyed saying it. We chatted a while about his career: early research in France and America, a holiday home on the Adriatic Coast which he could no longer visit. Given the choice, he would like to go back to America. Milan's dream was to sit in an air-conditioned seminar room on the West Coast, discussing supply side theory with New World sophomores.

The mid morning break was coming to an end. Milan pushed his metal chair back with a sharp scrape. What did I make of Serbia so far, he asked. Did I find people xenophobic? It was the first time someone had asked me that question. If people were hostile, I usually assumed it was because outsiders had provoked them, rather than from some innate local prejudice. Milan was less tolerant of his own kind.

"Do you read the horoscopes in *Politika*?" he asked.

Politika was Serbia's main daily paper, the official voice of President Milošević's government. I had to admit the horoscopes hadn't attracted my interest.

"You should," said Milan. "They're a way of whispering to the people. The editors know people don't read the news pages, so they put political messages in the horoscopes. You know, 'Foreign investments ahead' is a hint that sanctions are going to be lifted. 'Luck will come your way if you respect your family'. Well, that's just basic social control isn't it?"

Milan showed me to the stairs. I thanked him for returning my phone call: the first day's frenzy had not been entirely in vain.

All the same, I wondered whether I was looking in the right places. Another kind of Serbia existed behind the ministries and corporations: a country where larger truths emerged in astrology columns and homicidal folk songs. It was a matter of learning how to look.

The next morning, I was lying in bed watching a film on Serbia's First Channel. All the satellite stations were blank for some reason, so I was stuck with the local fare. Judging by the main character's wanton flares and raging moustache, the film was made in the mid 1970s. All in all, it was pretty feeble stuff: painter gets bad case of artist's block (marked by soft focus visuals and absurd stylophone noises). After a few days of beery angst he returns to his childhood home, hugs the forgotten parents and — hey, he's straight back to that blank canvas! Typical state art, I thought: a dumb story wrapped up in a docile message. Something else though held my attention: the sight and sound of Belgrade in another time, in Yugoslav time. The people looked different: they moved more confidently, looking forward, out of the screen. Their gestures had an open, engaged quality which was no longer there. Old films often offered this accidental pleasure: a hidden door into the recent past. Usually it provoked a brief shade of regret (the wish to be there rather than here). But what did you do when the past was unmistakably better than your soiled present. How did you live with that?

3 Freedom or Death

The posters appeared overnight: dark blue placards which showed Serbian and Russian flags nodding in harmony. Every spare wall and corrugated fence in the city seemed to have been covered. Beneath the flags there was a simple Cyrillic slogan:

> *Serbia, straighten up!*
> *Russia, wake up!*

It sounded more like a pitch for an aerobics class than for a political meeting, but as nationalist rallies in Serbia tended to slide into energetic violence, perhaps that was the point. I wanted to take a closer look at the phenomenon and here was an ideal opportunity. After a short absence, the extreme Russian nationalist Vladimir Zhirinovsky was heading back to town. Belgrade offered a congenial platform: any man whose idea of polite discussion was punching women MPs in the face would feel at home at the edge of Balkan politics. The event was being sponsored by the Serbian Radical Party, a group who shared many of Mr Zhirinovsky's thoughts and tastes. Their leader, Vojislav Šešelj — whose glaring features I had seen on the airport road a few days earlier — claimed the patriotic workout with Mr Zhirinovsky had a serious purpose. "The geostrategic position of the Serbs in the Balkans keeps deteriorating," he grumbled, "and the western powers and NATO are suppressing Serb national interests."

Šešelj's statement combined paranoia with bad history: his reference to Serbia's "geostrategic position" added a touch of bogus statesmanship. Foreign visitors had that kind of effect on the Radical Party leader: normally he was far more unreasonable. By the autumn of 1995, there was plenty for his supporters to be unreasonable about: they saw the Croatian victories and NATO bombardments as fresh evidence of Serbian betrayal. Krajina —

the historic Serb region in southern Croatia — had fallen to Croat forces in 72 hours: Belgrade had remained silent. President Milošević warned his former henchmen in Bosnia that Serbia was "not an ally worth counting on". The official media happily forgot this was the same man who had reportedly boasted in 1991 that Serbs may not know how to work, but "By God, we do at least know how to fight". Throughout September and October, Serb troops in Bosnia lost ground daily to the Croatian and Bosnian Army. In their political prime, the Radicals had summoned dreams of a "Greater Serbia": a domain which extended from Belgrade to the shores of the Adriatic. Defeat had drawn another kind of illusion in their cloudy heads: the fear of a "Greater Croatia" sketched out over the same land, like a negative version of the same mental plate.

Vladimir Zhirinovsky's flying visit would provide an opportunity to see whether ordinary Serbs felt the same way. At the time, his views carried a worrying weight: his Liberal Democratic Party was neither liberal nor democratic, but it was the largest party in the Russian parliament. (In the December 1995 elections, Zhirinovsky's party was relegated to second place behind the back-from-the-dead Communists. Even so, the Liberal Democrats remained strong enough to exert a malign sway over political life.) Zhirinovsky's calls for a strong, assertive Russia generated support at home and alarm almost everywhere else. Serbia however was one place where self-styled "Mad Vlad" could still win an audience. Sanctions meant Serbs were rather deprived on the entertainment front. Vladimir Zhirinovsky was a cheap alternative: comedian, lounge bar crooner and performing bear all rolled into one.

The posters told us to assemble outside the Federal Parliament at 5pm on October 20th. Dusk would give the rally a suitably melodramatic glow — as would its proximity to President Milošević's offices at the opposite end of Pioneer Park. The Serbian leader worked from a dour classical block topped by a clump of radio aerials. There was remarkably little visible security around the official residence. Two guards usually sat in a small plastic cabin; civilian cars could park within twenty metres of the main entrance. Fear though created its own aura: I never saw any sightseers around the Presidential palace. Maybe they were put off by the outsized pillars which made Milošević's residence look like an Athenian cast off.

An interesting confrontation looked on the cards until Belgrade's police department decided to ban the meeting. There were three days to go. A police spokesman said the Radical Party would "threaten the security of citizens and their property": a peculiar charge given that Serbia's leaders had once valued the Radicals for exactly that reason. During the Croatian and Bosnian wars, they had encouraged Šešelj and his homemade army to kick and punch non-Serbs out of their homes. No one would pay Šešelj's soldiers, so they paid themselves in stolen cars and swagged jewellery. These violent acts also served President Milošević's domestic policy. Šešelj — once dubbed Milošević's "remote control scarecrow" by local journalists — kept Serbs and international mediators clinging to the Serbian leader for fear of his rabid alternative.

Later that day, Šešelj replied with another press release. Dismissing the police arguments as "ridiculous", he vowed to march on the Federal Parliament despite the official ban. Similar boasts were made about a rally in the northern city of Novi Sad, where local authorities had also rolled up the red carpet. Šešelj's militant nationalism was being discarded by the Serbian authorities as swiftly as it had been created. Peace was spreading through the Balkans: all the newspapers said so.

While Šešelj considered how to amuse Mr Zhirinovsky in the police cells, I flicked through the newspapers. The horoscopes were short on advice, so I turned to some cheerful news from the industrial town of Niš. President Milošević, it was reported, had been awarded a Charter of Peace. The fact that this handy prize came from the local branch of his ruling Socialist Party did not seem to tarnish the honour. According to the citation, "Serbian President Slobodan Milošević received the charter for uniting Serbia, previously divided into three parts, for managing to save Serbia from falling on its knees in spite of sanctions, and for turning the Balkans from a gunpowder barrel into a peace polygon."

Belgrade's independent daily, *Naša Borba* (Our Struggle) had another story on its October 17th front page: "Rest of August pensions tomorrow."

Preparing for the rally (Mace alarm, shin pads and crash helmet), I tried to gather my thoughts on the Serb strain of nationalism. My own feelings towards patriotism and national pride were somewhat mixed. I accepted that everyone had the patriotic inflection to some degree or another: long spells away from Britain left me pining for the visual and verbal texture of home. Apart from family and friends, I missed newsprint, radio and TV, favourite places: the mental threads which form one's sense of here. Yet excessive displays of national ardour made me nervous. Some people will leave the room at the sight of a mouse or a spider. *Last Night of the Proms* did the same for me. Open Orwell's Room 101 and I would find swirling flags and jingoistic banners.

As a result, I found it hard at first to understand those who saw nationalism as the path to freedom, rather than a road away from it. On my first visit to Bosnia, I got talking with a soldier in the ski resort of Pale, the Bosnian Serbs' self-styled "capital". The soldier was loitering in a hotel car park, polishing a showroom-fresh silver Audi. He was about my age, and kitted out in black: a home made outfit probably run up on the family sewing machine. The uniform looked even odder than it sounds: until then, my only sight of Balkan blackshirts had been on the Croatian side. We started to talk about the war; he had lost brothers and cousins in the fighting. Was it all worth it, I wondered. "Of course !" the blackshirt insisted. "Because now I am truly free!"

There was a shrill edge to this thinking which I could not follow. Balkan patriotism was a desperate fusion of European nationalism and Russian nihilism. Before condemning such ideas outright, I tried to compare my circumstances with those of the bespoke soldier in the car park. My experiences had been distinctly different. For a start, the routines and loyalties were still intact. I had not been forced to enter Room 101, nor had I been compelled to make impossible choices. In Yugoslavia, people felt threatened and had talked themselves into extreme positions. War, when it came, did the rest. Dogmatic Serbs reduced it to a simple formula: *Sloboda ili Smrt*, Freedom or Death. Royalist Serbs — the "*četnici*" or Chetniks — had painted this slogan on their banners as they fought against Croatia's pro-Nazi regime in the early years of World War Two. According to the extremists, the only way to avenge an old crime was to commit a new one.

The respected ethnologist Ivan Čolović offered me some more thoughts. We met in his book-crammed apartment in New Belgrade. Čolović was a convinced Francophile, neatly turned out in a red corduroy shirt and faded jeans. Rather than do an interview, he lent me two of his recent research papers, "Undertones of War" and "The Political Myths of Ethnic Nationalism". First, Čolović stressed how the Yugoslav War was an artificial creation, a form of "mass transgression". Its aim was to make the destruction of one's enemy into "a sacred virtue." Equally important, political leaders had convinced their people that "war is always forced upon us, and is thus defensive." Killing had been elevated to an essential quality of the nation.

Second, Čolović explored the atavistic dimension of such conflicts. People were persuaded to see the war as a continuation of earlier struggles, a chance to revenge old losses. Thus, the Serbian obsession with avenging their defeat at Kosovo Polje in 1389 at the hands of the Ottoman Turks. The fact that many Albanians had fought alongside Serbs was forgotten in the rush to condemn. "War provides people with an opportunity to identify with their ancestors," wrote Čolović.

Such preoccupations help to create a new sense of time: one in which past and present exist in a continuum. The population starts to live in two places at once: in their troubled present and in the superior, collective past. Čolović concluded that in Serbia, "historical" time had been replaced by "mythical" time: an era of violent words and morbid acts. Myth had overtaken truth. The Serbian government had given this trend a sizeable shove. Celebrating the 600th anniversary of the Battle of Kosovo Polje in

1989, Serbia's President Milošević had declared: "Today it is difficult to know what is true and what is legend about the Battle of Kosovo. Today that is not even important."

Myths demanded sacrifices: the national cult of "*Serbie Céleste*", the immortal country, had been created. The most noble act was to die for your country. Čolović's articles outlined a moral universe within which an act of violence was seen as an act of justice. In a more simplistic form, these were the ideas which animated the nationalists of Belgrade or the soldiers in Srebrenica: the blindness of a cause, mythical time, the cult of one's ancestors. This was the frame in which people interpreted their actions. Čolović ended with a quotation from Marie Bonaparte: "Hatred in the heart of men is a capital which must be invested somewhere."

Aside from this manufactured mentality, I was beginning to see that the "threat" — as seen through Serb eyes — was partly a question of geography, and partly one of history. Serbs saw themselves as a threatened nation. As a landlocked state with no direct access to the sea, myths of conspiracy and outside interference found a ready audience. Isolation and occupation were ideal incubators: the idea of Serbs as uniquely suffering victims took hold. Past events — both factual and mythical — confirmed and embroidered these principles: Ottoman rule, the nineteenth-century push for independence, followed by a series of failed attempts at a common Yugoslav state. Viewed from a Balkan angle, nationalism was a natural craving for certainty and stability. It was how restive people on all sides reacted when the ground began to shift under their feet.

October 20th was cold, Belgrade's first autumn day. A small crowd of us had gathered on the breezy forecourt of the Inter Continental Hotel. The sky was filled with pearl clouds edged in white. Our hotel manager was there, a few feet in front of his shivering staff. He was a stout man with well-oiled black hair and a look of immense gloom on his face. I wasn't sure whether his discomfort was due to the changing weather or to the imminent ordeal of meeting Mr Zhirinovsky. Perhaps he was recalling the days when the Inter Continental welcomed a better class of celebrity. While we waited, a sharp wind rolled across the open driveway carrying the city's drab scent. Most places have a distinctive smell and Belgrade's was particularly depressing: a stagnant blend of petrol fumes, fried meat and stale cigarettes. The smell had already seeped through all my clothes, a calling card from the city.

Fifteen minutes late, a black Mercedes swung into the hotel driveway, a Russian flag quivering from its long bonnet. The manager checked the knot of his tie. After a short delay, the back door opened and a creased figure landed on the pavement. Mr Zhirinovsky straightened up and mopped his chin with a white handkerchief. His pudgy face was set in a theatrical scowl: eyebrows lowered and mouth drawn down as if stifling a persistent belch. Common lore says that people look better in real life than in photographs, but here was someone who looked decidedly worse in the flesh than he ever did on camera.

"Welcome to Belgrade," said the manager.

Mr Zhirinovsky mumbled some blurred Russian in reply.

Patting his flat curls back into place, the Russian politician walked past the manager and into his hotel. Everyone stood and watched: there was a sense that something was supposed to happen here, but no one was quite sure what. In my notebook I wrote: "An occasion in search of a reason." Mr Zhirinovsky was dressed in a grey double-breasted suit and tan slip-on shoes. He seemed to think a steady procession was the best way to impress his Serbian audience. Instead, the sweaty curls and half-mast tie gave him the appearance of a drunken uncle at a rural wedding.

Our host, Vojislav Šešelj, had also smartened up for the day. His impressive belly was tucked into a dark blue suit with matching tartan tie. I looked for the manager but he had vanished along with his staff. It was a bit early in the day for a punch up, though one could never be sure. I checked the exits. Šešelj was frowning: behind his steel-framed glasses, the Radical Party leader looked upset. Zhirinovsky was wheeling about too, mumbling to himself.

After a brief chat, the two men made for a vacant table staked out with a Radical Party pennant. I tried to follow them and found my path blocked by an odd looking man with a twirly moustache and monocle.

"Keep back!" he shouted. "Security cordon !"

Sure enough, a row of block-headed heavies had surrounded the two leaders, enclosing them in a human stockade. It was an intimidating and rather pointless display: apart from myself, the only people left in reception were a couple of cleaners hoovering the carpet. Mr Twirly Moustache would give no quarter, so I retreated to the main desk. Inside their pen, the two statesmen were having a half-hearted conversation about how Serbia had been betrayed by Milošević and how patriotic Serbs should fight back, etc, etc. No one appeared to be listening to this stale dialogue, and judging by the bored expressions on their faces, neither participant was paying much attention either.

One of the bellboys was still at his counter, sneaking a cigarette. I asked him what was going on.

"They're waiting for the cameras," he said.

Šešelj always damned the media for misrepresenting him, yet without their electronic seal this event did not seem to be taking place. The charade went on for several more minutes before Vladimir and Vojislav began to flag. Zhirinovsky slouched in his plum leather seat and stared out of the high windows. To while away the time, Šešelj opened a plastic folder and ran through the Great Russian's travel arrangements. Mr Twirly Moustache coughed and yawned.

All of a sudden there was a yelp of brakes. Two estate cars careered into the hotel's parking bay, ejecting a handful of shabby men with lenses. The security guards squared their shoulders. As the cameras zoomed and panned, the two leaders discovered a new and intense interest in each other's company. Šešelj talked with actorish gusto about Geostrategy and the Pan-Slav Axis. Zhirinovsky stretched out his arms and legs, as if lying in a jacuzzi. Seeing as he was normally photographed in that sort of environment, it looked natural enough.

The cameramen puffed and grunted. I stood next to one of the stills photographers, a fat fellow wearing a canvas jacket riddled with pockets and pouches.

"Interesting?" I volunteered.

"Nah," he said. It was a local accent shaded with the standard American burr.

"He's a shit, a big shit," he added.

"Which one?"

"Both of them."

The photographer replaced his lens cap. We had waited almost half an hour for a two minute photo call. I showed him the official programme.

"What's happening next?" I asked.

"Nothing's happening next. Until further notice."

"What about the programme?"

The cameraman laughed.

"They're completely behind on that. It's all going wrong." With that, he waddled back to his car.

After a few more minutes, the other shooters and snappers came to the same conclusion. Sensing their time was over, Šešelj and Zhirinovsky walked stiffly to the lifts, their actions directed by two insistent cameramen. Once Zhirinovsky had stepped into the elevator, the camera lights were switched off, leaving Šešelj forlorn in the lobby darkness.

Quarter to five. The taxi driver spotted them first. We were heading downtown across Brankova bridge, when he saw three policemen standing at the roadside. They weren't doing much: just smoking cigarettes and strolling about, hands in camouflage pockets. Fifty metres on, a second group was clustered round a blue and white patrol car, radios crackling. Their pistols were dimly visible under the amber street lights. My stomach gave a nervy twinge: Belgraders were good at demonstrations. Unfortunately, so were the police.

We reached the city's Orthodox Cathedral, a vaulting mass with a distant dome. Word had gone out that the march would be setting off from here, and around seven to eight hundred people had gathered in the dusk. Elbowing my way through the crowd, it looked like a fairly jumbled mob. Hard faced country men in felt hats stood next to city couples in business suits and pastel raincoats. The only key to their common allegiance was a small metal version of the double headed Serbian eagle, the *Kokarda*, attached to every lapel. Flags swayed everywhere: Serbia's national banner was simply Yugoslavia's old blue, white and red stripes with the star extracted from its heart.

The road was kept clear by a line of party officials. Most of them had the gruff docility of ex-soldiers; some were veterans of the Second World War rather than the current conflict. A handful even looked wild enough to remember Archduke Franz Ferdinand's last trip around Sarajevo. One ageing warrior was holding up a hand drawn poster from his home town: SMEDEREVO SAYS STAND UP SERBIA AGAINST THE NEW WORLD ORDER! The point was reinforced by helpful sketches — in fluorescent yellow — of Russia and Serbia. Somehow the ex-Superpower and the Balkan state had ended up the same size. Maybe there was some truth in that old Serbian folk song, *Who is the liar that says Serbia is small?*

A younger soldier swung by on wooden crutches. He wore a neat battlefield outfit and was a regular at these events. I'd seen his angry red face in a file of archive photographs and remembered his bitter features. The soldier had been snapped wobbling past a woman peace protestor: she looked on haughtily, dangling a carrot over his head at the end of a long rod.

Biding their time, the crowd started to chant. The words *Serbia — Russia* hammered around the streets, picking up speed and volume. *Sir-bee-yah, Roo-see-yah!* I made for the cathedral steps, close to the photographers and TV crews. It felt safer there. I'd come along with Dada, an old friend. She was used to these kind of marches and stood around flicking her auburn hair in a bored fashion. Dada was short for Dragana, though I'd never worked out why.

"Two things you've got to remember about these kind of meetings," she drawled. "First, try and stick up at the front with the leaders, in case, you know, the police attack the back."

"Uh-huh," I said, cool as anything.

"And second, don't get too close to the TV cameras either."

"Why?"

"Because the Radicals sometimes try and beat up the cameramen."

So there it was: get pulped by the police or mashed by the no-brainers. It was good to have a choice. Dada took a practical approach. She stared down at her full length dress and Timberland walking boots.

"I hope we don't have to run," she giggled. "I'm not very well dressed."

A squat youth in a purple suit was listening to our conversation. Our press tags had caught his interest, as had my notebook. After working out that I was British, or probably American, he treated me to an unpleasant stare: half sulk, half snarl. Some people still resented the NATO air raids. I moved further up the cathedral steps and sheltered next to a smartly dressed woman, turned out in navy blue jacket and pink knitted skirt.

"How many people here do you think?" I said.

She smiled. Her hair was cut in a black bob.

"Well, I'd say a few thousand already," she said. "But of course, a lot of people will join us as we walk."

Her English was precise and, for a change, English accented. She spoke with such conviction that it seemed pointless to contradict. My new friend was from Kragujevac, a large town south of Belgrade, "in the heart of Serbia" as she put it. We went on looking at the crowd for a few moments and then I asked whether she'd seen Mr Zhirinovsky before.

"Oh yes. It was my pleasure to meet him at the airport," she trilled. "He's brilliant, a real Russian nationalist. He's the leader of the best party in Russia."

"How long have you been in the Radicals?"

"Oh, I've been a member of the party since it started four years ago," she said proudly. "Now I'm President of my area."

The crowd were getting noisier: *Sir-bee-yah, Roo-see-yah! Sir-bee-yah, Roo-see-yah!* The President of Kragujevac had a Chanel-style ruched handbag and a silver *Kokarda* on her lapel.

"What's the point of the Radicals?" I asked. "After all, Milošević doesn't want you any more."

The President shook her bobbed head.

"Oh no," she said. "This party does everything for the Serbian people. We've brought market reforms to Serbia, and we're supporting the Serbian people."

She trailed off and turned towards the crowd.

"Milošević and his party are dictators with no idea of democracy," she said finally, as if reading off a press release. We could agree on that point, though I suspected she wanted rather more of the dictatorship and a little less of the democracy. Beneath us, there was one sure sign our heroes had arrived: the camera lights had been turned on, their twitchy beams pricking the sky.

"I think they're here," she said firmly, keen to end our conversation. With a brief nod, the President of Kragujevac turned to applaud her two leaders as they fought their way into the cathedral. Under the floodlights, Zhirinovsky looked rather more alert than at his morning debut, a wide smile on his lips. An elderly woman grabbed him by the lapels and planted a kiss on his dappled cheek. Šešelj edged his way forward, shaking stray hands for the benefit of photographers.

After a brief service, the two men bolted back into the crowd, this time surrounded by tubby bodyguards. With another round of *Serbia — Russia*, the mass began to shift and change form.

"To the parliament! To the parliament!" they shouted. Dada took my arm. Now this was the point when I should, on balance, have gone back to the hotel. I toyed with the idea of telling Dada that I really had to leave: there was a relatively new episode of *Star Trek — The Next Generation* on German telly and anything was better than this. *Last Night of the Proms* was ugly enough when inflicted down a TV tube, but a night out with the Serbian Radical Party was a thousand times worse. Imagine "Rule Britannia" with firearms rather than car horns and you'll get close enough.

We began to head north, past the shuttered cafes and offices on 7th July Street. People were walking fast, bawling names and waving banners. There was a sense of crazed urgency pushing us through the cold evening air. A new chant went up as we stomped along : *We are the Chetniks! Come out of your houses!* A black flag decorated with a skull and crossbones waggled above our heads: *Sloboda ili Smrt,* Freedom or Death.

Zhirinovsky and Šešelj were about a hundred metres ahead, lauded by artificial light. This seemed the right kind of place to be: neither too far back, or too close to the front. I looked at the faces around us. We had drawn level with a hank of teenage boys kitted out in standard Serbian retro chic: designer track suits and chunky Orthodox crosses. With glazed anger they shouted their favourite Milošević one liners: *Slobo, you bastard, you've betrayed the Krajina* and *Milošević, you Ustaša whore* — a reference to the pro-Nazi regime in Croatia during the Second World War.

They chanted without much skill or passion. There was a trance-like quality to this performance which I found unnerving. Everyone seemed to be going through a familiar ritual, something which had to be done, an accepted way to let off political steam. This was how things were done in mythical Serbia. We entered Belgrade's main shopping street, Knez Mihailova. People were being sucked in from the sidewalk as if by some hidden force. Passing a department store, I noticed a young man in denims watching the crowd. Sensing a gap, he dived in to the marching mob, a childish smile on his face. He looked happier: self-determination for this group was a form of self-annihilation.

The Federal Parliament was five minutes away but my stomach was already there, anticipating the grief to come. Our group of marchers were gearing up with a slight improvisation: *Slobo, you motherfucker, you've betrayed the Krajina.* At the eastern end of Knez Mihailova, I spotted a thick line of militia men blocking the route. My insides went into a heavy spin. Belgrade demonstrations usually ended this way: with childish chants and bruises in the dark.

My notes got rather incoherent at this stage: single words like SCREAM and SPEED wobbled across the page. But then I had my head down most of the time, wondering whether I would ever see home again, let alone the new series of *Star Trek.* As a result, it took a few minutes for me to realise that we had changed direction. Amid the genteel cafes of Republic Square, the march had taken a sharp turn to the left, and moved off towards the National Museum. Early evening diners froze at their plates as we rumbled past. Such was my relief at the cancelled scrap, that I felt no embarrassment as we marched through the rush hour traffic. Someone said we were making for the Radical Party's headquarters in Francuska Street, and that was good enough for me. Our parade seemed to amuse the idling motorists: a teenage girl sat, arms crossed, at the wheel of her vintage Fiat as we swarmed over and around her car. A silver birdcage lay on the front passenger seat.

After a long walk down a dark street, we reached the Radical Party's offices, a golden-yellow building with stucco frills. Feeble whistles punctuated the slogan shouting: there was a general sense of defeat, of a missed opportunity. I seemed to be the only one who thought that, on the whole, this was rather a splendid turn of events.

There were some muted calls of "Lead us, Lead us" and the two leaders came out on a balcony, helpfully lit by the constant camera lights. Seen from below, it looked like a scene from some gaslit Victorian music hall: an impression compounded by the cheerless whiff of sweat and cigarettes. Vojislav Šešelj spoke first, his bass boom needing no amplification. "Brother and Sister Serbs," he shouted. "Whenever we have had hard times in the past, we could always rely on Russia." It was an imaginative resumé of Yugoslav-Soviet relations during the Cold War, but perhaps this was not the best time to point it out.

"Milošević thinks he has banned our meeting," he went on. "But he cannot ban us from anything."

There was a half-hearted cheer and a scatter of boos.

Vladimir Zhirinovsky stepped forward, clasping his fists above his head like a fairground fighter. Compared to Šešelj, his voice sounded thin and mousy. "The time of traitors in Russia is now over," he squeaked, "Serbs are now Russia's priority." The mob cheered and helpfully twirled their three-fingered Serb salute for the cameras.

"We are going to win over our enemies," he continued, "through the brotherly feeling between Russia and Serbia." There was a louder cheer this time and one ragged verse of a Chetnik song. Šešelj and Zhirinovsky stood awkwardly on the balcony and waved to the crowd. No one was quite sure what should happen next: Radical Party meetings were not strong on etiquette. Once again the media made the decision for them. After a few more chants, the camera lights were doused and the leaders went back inside. Francuska Street returned to its evening shadow.

Dada lit a cigarette. My watch said 5.47.

"Is that it?" I said.

"That's it. Can we go now?"

Deprived of its electronic stage, the crowd quickly drained away. People got back to their lives. I wondered what had happened to the hollering teenagers, the grinning bystander in denim. What had they turned into during the march, and what would they revert back to? The rally had been a tolerable disappointment: I had feared a lot worse.

As we walked back up Francuska Street, Dada met a friend of her parents, a middle-aged woman dressed in furs. She looked rather embarrassed to have been caught at such a meeting. While we talked, she scratched the bridge of her nose.

"How many people here do you think?" Dada asked her.

"About ten thousand," said the woman, and laughed nervously. "It all depends on your sources."

Back at the hotel that night, I tried to take stock. The rally had really been several events at once: part political protest, part street ruck with a sprinkle of religious ritual. In Britain, one usually got the first and second ingredients, but rarely the third. Religion still overlapped with politics in this part of Europe. The Orthodox faith brought a sense of mission to the Serbian cause: it also provided a moral language for the national project. Spiritual and temporal had fused into an exalted whole. I had seen the same phenomenon on the Croat side: one of the first acts carried out by Croats after taking Knin was to hold a Catholic service above the town.

The Belgrade marchers saw their actions in the same abstract, idealistic context. Their world view had its own kind of logic, albeit one that I found repellent and somewhat incoherent. In their eyes, the Radicals were the political heirs to the Chetnik tradition: they shared the same historical territory.

Again, we were back to time. The past had a density, an active presence which coloured every action. I had seen the flags, the *Kokarda* on every lapel. Orthodox precepts emphasised the cyclical nature of life: what had been done before would come round again. People regarded the present not as a unique experience in itself, but merely as an extra part of the past, an expected addition. There had been an air of glum compulsion about the event too, a kind of ancestral pressure. Serbs saw themselves as a unique breed, yet I also sensed a people buckling under the weight of their own dreams.

The rally had affected me in other ways. For an hour or so afterwards, my voice and gestures were far louder than usual. Maybe I had enjoyed the experience more than I cared to admit (the escape into crowds, all that mobbish power!). I was also relieved that it was over. Another chunk of earthly time had passed. Normal time was much more tedious and heavy than its mythical counterpart. We had filled another day under embargo.

4   A Man from the Nineteenth Century

I decided not to follow Šešelj and Zhirinovsky to Novi Sad. The meeting promised a repeat performance of what we had seen in Belgrade and I was looking forward to an idle weekend. Having spent some time with the activists, I wanted to examine the thinking behind the nationalist movement. How had the ground been prepared? A day later, I heard that the Novi Sad rally had broken down into street fights and arrests, thus confirming my winning talent for missing the story. I drew some faint comfort from the fact there wasn't much about it in the Belgrade press either: *Politika* was more concerned with diplomacy. America's latest Yugoslav envoy, Richard Holbrooke, was shuttling around the Balkans with a new peace plan. The prospect so excited *Politika* that it came up with an unintentionally comic headline: "PEACE IS INEVITABLE". Only in the Balkans, one was tempted to say, did peace sound like a new type of threat. As usual, the real reason behind these pacific overtures was buried on the inside pages. Bosnian Serb forces had lost Drvar and Sanski Most to the Bosnian/Croat army. Prijedor — and even Banja Luka — could fall next. "The Bosnian Serbs now control 48.4 per cent of Bosnia-Hercegovina," reported the United Nations, "and the Bosnian/Croat Army hold 51.6 per cent." Clearly, it was better to sue for peace while this figure was tolerably close to the fifty per cent mark.

Serbia's national project was being squeezed from within and without: I wanted to get some sense of the ideas behind the dream in case it disappeared altogether. I ruled out politicians: the important ones never talked and the rest talked too much. I was looking for someone with decided opinions on the conflict, and on nationalism in particular. One name kept coming up, so I decided to give him a call.

Momo Kapor was a novelist and painter, a well known figure on the Belgrade arts scene for almost thirty years. He was also one of Serbia's leading propagandists: a born-again fount of national hatred. During the Bosnian war, he had written a weekly newspaper column "XX weeks under embargo": where X was the number of weeks Serbia had lived under the "unjust and unwarranted" sanctions. Kapor's column mixed personal anecdotes with patriotic tirades. In effect, he had helped cultivate the moral atmosphere which made the war possible. Kapor had little time for liberals, and they in turn had scant love for him. A recording of the author's rambling thoughts about women and wartime was gleefully broadcast by Radio B92, Belgrade's bravest radio station.

Equally striking had been Kapor's furious attacks on Sarajevo. He defended the Serb decision to surround and shell the city — and even visited the front lines as a self-styled "War Correspondent". "Kapor's hatred of Sarajevo has reached a psychotic level," said Alex, a bookish friend. "It's even more bizarre when you realise he was born there."

Milena the academic took another view. She understood Kapor in a way, even though she hated him. "Like most Serbs born in Bosnia and Croatia, he sees the Serbian national question as the crucial question," she said. "That makes a huge difference to his perspective." Kapor embodied the central failure of Yugoslavia : how to accommodate the Serbian diaspora in Bosnia and Croatia. Like thousands of other Serbs, Kapor was a member of a minority and a majority at the same time, as journalist Vesna Pesić explained. "When you are a minority you become very militant," she wrote in 1992. "When you become a majority you become very arrogant. There is no experience of a mature majority."

During the late Sixties and early Seventies, Kapor had won a reputation as an innovator, a modern "Yugoslav" kind of artist. I wondered how the revolutionary had become a reactionary, why time had been thrown back. Kapor's journey mirrored that of his contemporaries. On the phone he was friendly enough. I was to come over at eleven in the morning, and we would take it from there.

*

The apartment was in Skadarlija, Belgrade's bohemian quarter. We sat at one end of a long white room, surrounded by canvasses. Most of the paintings on display were of a slightly aloof looking woman whom I took to be the writer's wife. There were two more works in progress on a large easel by the window. For these portraits, the model had been turned into a floral Medusa, her hair studded with lilac wreaths. Both heads hung alarmingly in the painted air, as if impaled on spikes.

The real Mrs Kapor had met us at the door. She shared the same fine features as the paintings, though not the high manner which the artist appeared to find there. She was much younger than her husband, who was in his late fifties. This morning, she was carrying a tennis racket under one arm: a match at midday, she explained.

Momo Kapor watched this activity from an old leather armchair.

"I met her on an aeroplane," he said. "She was an air stewardess then."

Mrs Kapor smiled tolerantly. Her husband was dressed down in a blue check Lacoste shirt and a pair of Levi's jeans which hung loosely around his thin legs. Grey hair parted in several directions over his sallow face. Kapor claimed that on a recent visit to New York, a passer-by had mistaken him for Ralph Lauren. I found that rather hard to credit, even among star-hungry New Yorkers. More amusing was Kapor's evident pride at having been compared with a Yankee fashion guru. But then fame works both ways: if Ralph Lauren came to Belgrade, he'd probably get dragged into a bar and asked how the new novel was going.

Kapor spoke in a thick baritone, pausing now and then for a nervous giggle. When I played back my tape recording later on, his laugh was everywhere: a pizzicato hiss like an overactive bike pump. His English wasn't too great ("It's only good enough to order food and chat up girls," he said), so Dada's identical twin sister Dubravka had come along to help. The twins looked and sounded so much alike that they often stood in for each other at dull parties. Dubravka was known as Duda.

"I've lived all over the world," he began. "But one of the consequences of this war is that I've started being xenophobic."

"Why?"

"Because we believe the whole western world is against us. Of course it could be paranoia. It reminds me of the story about the policeman who's chasing a man down the street. The man stops and turns to the policeman and says: 'If you don't stop chasing me, I'll get persecution mania'."

He chuckled.

"The way I see it, it's very simple. The New World Order is a complete fiction. It's against the country I belong to and the country I live in."

I assumed he meant Serb-held Bosnia and Serbia respectively. Mrs Kapor came in with a tray of Turkish coffee, giving her husband an excuse to light the first in a long chain of Kent cigarettes.

"This is not paranoia," he puffed. "This is the truth."

"But Serbs are in a worse position now than when the war started."

Kapor nodded.

"So what was the point of it all," I went on. "The project has failed, the Serbs are divided again."

"Ah, you know the division of Serbs is an old Serbian syndrome," he said confidently, as if this clinched the argument. "It's a curse we've had for more than 500 years. But I'm an optimist. When you lose some battles, it doesn't mean you've lost the war. After all, people live for a long time: one hundred years in the life of a people is just like a moment. It's pretty bad for our lives because we don't live for one hundred years, but we should look ahead. A nation and its people cannot be destroyed."

We were back in the mythical past. History condemned Serbs to their unique fate; individuals were as nothing when compared to the long march of national liberation. Political struggles across the world drew on the same rhetoric: projects carried out in the name of the people, yet with no room for them in their final design. The past was used to pardon the excesses of the present. Srebrenica's executioners saw themselves as on a mission to assert national rights. Yet Serbs had made themselves victims twice over. They saw themselves as martyrs throughout history. Now they had become the prime victims of their own ambitions.

"Serbs are people who can make victories from their defeats," Kapor went on. "For example, the greatest victory in Serbian history was the Battle of Kosovo in 1389. Psychologically, we need to know how to make victory out of defeat."

Mrs Kapor reappeared, dressed in a white track suit. After a whispered farewell she left for her tennis game, abandoning the room where she had been so tirelessly celebrated in oil and ink. Momo Kapor downed his coffee with a satisfied smack of the lips.

"History here is repeating itself all the time," he said. "This is a very old area: the movie has been shown over and over again. People who come here and make decisions about us — I'm talking about people who come from the western world — come here without being prepared. They don't know much about our traditions here, or about our culture."

There was a defensive edge to Kapor's answers which I found slightly unusual. He seemed to be having an argument with himself: self-conscious enough to know these were unpopular opinions, yet unable to stop them coming out. Perhaps that helped explain the nervy laughter. Self-hatred would be too strong a term, though there was a strong sense of unease at what he had become.

"Look at another thing," he added. "When we talk about 'Greater Serbia'" — at this point Kapor wiggled his index fingers for ironic punctuation — "you shouldn't have anything against that if you come from Great Britain. Nobody's really bothered about that, are they?"

"How would you describe yourself?"

"I'm a Serbian nationalist, and I don't find anything bad in that. If you open up a dictionary and look up the word 'Nationalist' you'll see that it's a French word. The French thought of it, you know, not the Serbs."

The author let out a triumphant sniff, as if he had scored a vital point.

"Translate it literally," he went on, "and you'll find it means someone who loves their country, a patriot. A man who is fighting for the interests of his people."

"Not everyone is like that."

"Sure. But a nationalist is not the same as a chauvinist you know. That's a type of character from French drama. Look, every person in Great Britain is a nationalist. It's very normal."

We were heading towards a familiar argument. By pushing me into a patriotic corner, Kapor wanted to make a direct link between Balkan nationalism and the West European strain. Our conversation came to a halt. Beneath us, pavement restaurants were limbering up for lunch: loud folk music welled up through the netted windows. It was past midday. Momo Kapor jumped to his feet, the first time he'd moved since we had arrived, save for the constant task of pulling a cigarette in and out of his mouth.

"I think it's time for a drink," he said, and strode over to a glass fronted cabinet full of white china plates. Bending down, he opened a small cupboard and produced a flask sized bottle of Ballantine's whisky. With his spare hand, Kapor fingered three frosted tumblers and brought them over to our wooden table with a barman's skill.

"Heh heh!" he said.

It had to happen sooner or later. The moment I had feared, when my drinking problem would be exposed. For reasons too tedious to repeat, I had stopped drinking almost two years ago after a long illness. Balkan folk found my decision hard to understand: the trait of a misanthrope, a dry sociopath. Serbs thought I was the one with the drinking difficulty. Our host though took the refusal with a worldly grunt and tipped my imagined portion into Duda's glass.

"Heh heh!"

Kapor helped himself to a triple, the whisky splashing round his crystal glass. After a relieved gasp, he turned back to our conversation. He seemed to be having second thoughts, sensing that his words had gone too far.

"Don't misunderstand me," he said. "I have a lot of friends among Croatian writers. My publisher was in Zagreb until this war."

As he talked and gurgled, I tried to imagine what Momo Kapor had been like in his beloved past, the place where all excuses can be found. I wanted to know how he had got here, how he had fallen into this frame of mind. Before the war, his renown as a writer of hardboiled novels had been enlarged by a series of television hymns to his beloved Dubrovnik. Viewers saw their favourite writer sharing an aperitif with Croatian friends, a model of Yugoslav brotherhood and unity. When the war started, Kapor the Croat-lover mutated into a fierce Croat-hater, crowing over the Federal Army's attacks on the medieval town and its surroundings.

For a while, we talked about favourite writers, which seemed like safe common ground. Our loud host reminded me of an Angry Young Man gone sour: a familiar British sort, salted with Balkan spleen. He loved what he dubbed "the little great authors" of English realism: writers like Alan Sillitoe, John Braine and Stan Barstow. Kapor had emerged as a relatively experimental voice in the 1960s, writing realistic stories about everyday life. Serbia's cultural inner circle did not warm to his earthy tales, though they were popular with a wider public. He became a bestseller, popular right across the former Yugoslavia. Recognition brought TV and radio commissions, newspaper columns and a welcome celebrity. Even so, I wondered how the cool attitudes of his artistic peers had affected him. Rejection turns some people against their chosen dream. Kapor though seemed to come into another category: those for whom exclusion merely heightened the drive for recognition, the wish to belong.

We talked about Sarajevo: the history of the city and how Kapor had left as a nine-year-old. Until now, our conversation had been fairly even-tempered, but Sarajevo summoned a harsher tone. I recalled Elie Kedourie's description of early nineteenth-century nationalists, speaking with "indignant eloquence." The laughter came less frequently. After a series of general prejudices we had suddenly moved to the specific and the particular.

"I was born in Sarajevo," he said. "And I see that as something enriching, not something bad. In my childhood, I listened to Bach's *Fugues* in the Catholic cathedral and to Muslim priests at the mosque."

"So were you upset by what happened to the city?"

Kapor snorted.

"No. My job is not to be upset. It's to understand. As for me and Sarajevo, well I was sure all this would happen over twenty years ago. But I was banned from the city by the Communist regime. For twenty-three years I could not visit my town because they would arrest me, or kill me 'by accident'. I was not the only one saying this, by the way."

Momo Kapor, it turned out, was friends with the Bosnian Serbs' political leader, Radovan Karadži ć. He admitted to this with a proud wink. Before the war, Dr Karadž i ć had practised psychiatry in Sarajevo and pursued a second career as a poet. In both fields, he too had been snubbed by the University élite. There was another symmetry here: two men excluded from their chosen ambitions, both with an exaggerated sense of nationhood.

Kapor drained his tumbler. As we talked, he took the ashtray out to the kitchen and tipped its contents into a smart plastic dustbin.

"What do you mean by persecution?" I asked.

"First of all," he shouted from the kitchen, "one of my plays was forbidden. It had won all the possible awards at different festivals. Then they banned everything that I said in interviews. They wanted to arrest me as the enemy."

Kapor's account struck me as rather confused. He wanted to cast himself as victim and perpetrator at the same time. We had moved into bitter, private territory. Returning to the table, Kapor laid the clean ashtray next to a refreshed glass. His voice assumed a whining, sarcastic tone.

"You know of course, Sarajevo was living a fake existence at that time? There was the Olympics, 'Brotherhood and Unity'. Everything was *nice*. Underneath, you know, an evil was sleeping. And this evil is always sensed by the artist."

He paused, tumbler in hand.

"Artists have special senses. And Radovan Karadžić was the first to sense this. Take a look at all the personalities in this drama, as if they're in a police line up. You need to figure out who's the killer, who's committed all the rapes, yes?"

I shrugged my shoulders and looked down. Kapor's impression of the Bosnian Serb leader did not square with my own. Karadžić had been indicted by the United Nations War Crimes Tribunal for crimes against humanity; for ordering the persistent, deranged shelling of Sarajevo and for helping to plan the massacre of up to eight thousand men in Srebrenica.

"Anthropologically, you need to look at the construction of the face and the body," Kapor went on. "And then you'll see that Radovan Karadžić is the only civilized person there."

He leant forward in the armchair, suddenly animated.

"Take a look at Izetbegović, the Bosnian President. You can see that syphilis and fanaticism are within him from the construction of his face."

"And what do you see in Dr Karadžić's face?"

"First of all, a deep understanding of the tragedy. I can see that he's suffering. I see a lot of nobility in him too."

I'm not sure exactly when we parted company during this conversation. Maybe it was Kapor's vision of the historic Serbian project or his sneering account of Sarajevo. By the time he started to divine character from faces, I had withdrawn altogether. Beneath all the rhetoric about national destiny and the Serbian mission, this was what Kapor's ideas came down to: a petulant confection of pseudo science and stupefying bigotry. For a moment, I thought the reference to facial features was an ill-judged joke, some kind of rag for the visiting liberal. Kapor's face though remained serious: there were no second thoughts or defensive sniggers. I couldn't connect at all: Kapor knew that, and seemed to be enjoying my discomfort.

"Do you remember the name of the road where you were born?" he said, changing the subject.

I nodded.

"How many times has that name been changed since then?"

"Never."

"Exactly. Like Fifth Avenue or Madison Avenue, yes?"

"Probably." I didn't want to get involved. I wanted to wrap this up. Soon.

"Well here's my story," he went on. "This will help you understand. I was born on the main street in Sarajevo — a road which history has crossed many times. When I was born in 1937, it was called King Alexander Street. During the Second World War, it was renamed Ante Pavelić Street (the wartime Croatian leader installed by Nazi Germany). After the war it became Marshall Tito street — and during this war, it's been renamed after a black marketeer. The name has changed four times during my life."

The ground had shaken under Momo Kapor's feet. This was how he and thousands of nervous Serbs — particularly those on the fringes — had responded. Kapor's anecdote reminded me of an episode in Fitzroy Maclean's *Eastern Approaches*. Entering the Bosnian town of Bugojno in 1944, Maclean received a crash course in recent Balkan history. "Like every town and village in Bosnia it had been fought over a score of times in the past two years and was largely in ruins," he wrote:

> On its poor bullet-scarred white-washed walls [there were] the inscriptions of the previous occupants: MUSSOLINI HA SEMPRE RAGIONE; EIN VOLK, EIN REICH, EIN FÜHRER, had been crossed out and replaced in flaming red paint by the slogan of the Partisans; ŽIVIO TITO; SMRT FASCISMU, SLOBODA NARODU — Long Live Tito. Death to Fascism. Liberty to the People. If you looked carefully you could see that the still earlier Partisan inscriptions of a previous occupation had been painted out by the Germans when the village had changed hands before.

At one point, Kapor had taken a tour of Serbian front lines above Sarajevo. Through a pair of military binoculars, he had watched fellow Serbs shell the street on which he was born.

"My choice was formulated by the novelist Ivo Andrić," he said. "His motto was: 'A writer should always be with his people, even when his people are not right.' What am I supposed to do?

Am I supposed to write like James Joyce, like he did in *Finnegan's Wake*? No."

"You mean it's impossible to write like that in these kind of situations?"

"No, it is possible. But there are different types of writers."

"So what kind of writer are you?"

"We're coming to the basic question now."

"In what way?"

"Well, if my father's house was attacked, or even the house of my grandfather, or the houses of all my relatives, then what am I supposed to do? To write like Proust in *A la recherche du temps perdu* — or go there and see what's happening. You could lose your head, but you must be there to see what is happening to your relatives, and to be at their side."

He released a flume of edgy laughter.

"You know, it's a shocking thing to say, but war is only useful for novelists and nobody else. In war, all passions are naked. It's the epicentre of the human drama. You hear about so many dramas that you cannot write them all."

The second tumbler of whisky had kicked in. Kapor was starting to wave his hands around and his voice had swelled to a shout.

"A few days ago, I was in Rome to see my eldest daughter. She's a well known Italian painter you know. She held a party in my honour and..." — Kapor's lip curled — "lots of *nice* people turned up.

"Somebody there asked me what was happening in the Bosnian War, because it was the lead story every night on their TV news programmes. So I started to talk, and then I realised that I was talking louder than everybody else. I talked about destroyed towns, the massive exodus, all the battles I'd been to. And they looked at me with amazement! They didn't understand. They thought I was a man from the nineteenth century."

"Why were you talking so loudly?"

"Because I'm alive and they're not. They live a very boring Rome life: going to art galleries, spending money. That's the worst kind of world. I used to belong to it, but now I've forgotten it. Look at those people in Geneva! They're all dead. It's just that no one has certified them yet."

Kapor's Sarajevo sneer had come back again. We had strayed onto another classic nationalist theme: the superiority of native culture over idle cosmopolitanism. Such claims came strangely from Kapor. Earlier, he had boasted of living "all over the world", exhibiting his paintings in Boston and New York. The only common strand between these two positions was the desire to impress. The idea that Balkan lives were more vivid, more soulful than West European ones was another traditional and faintly desperate argument. Many of Momo Kapor's fellow citizens would take the opposite view: glad to exchange Balkan colour for a dull peace. But then I also remembered some of the impressionistic arguments I had used to justify my interest in the region: that it was somehow more "real", more unpredictable than life at home. What were the sources of that attraction? I suspected journalists were drawn here in part because it was tolerably exotic: close enough in climate and general history to feel familiar, yet also absorbingly strange. We were in a land of seers and mendicants, magicians and fools. If that was how I saw the Balkans, then I could hardly chide Momo Kapor for celebrating the same qualities. I wondered why he so despised his neighbours in Italy.

"Because there are no surprises," he said earnestly. "Everyone knows what pension they're going to get, what car they're going to buy. They live in a system where everything is known. By contrast, the life depicted by Shakespeare is completely unpredictable. And that is life. Full of dangers, full of passion. Full of love, full of hate."

"They're not all like that."

Kapor laughed.

"Yes, but take Switzerland," he said. "Nobody hates each other but then again, nobody loves each other either."

I looked at my watch. The day had slipped from mid morning to mid afternoon, a bleary journey into Kapor's imagined world. Over four hours, his combative streak had turned into fanatical sourness. Kapor's ideas had been supported by examples of snubs and disappointments. Perhaps that rage filled the silence when words ran dry. I started to make vague hints about winding up the conversation, hints which made Kapor unhappy.

"You know, I don't normally agree to meet journalists," he snapped. "I only agreed to see you because you're writing a book."

I thanked him for his time and cooperation.

"I feel like the credits are beginning to run at the end of this programme," he grumbled. "I suppose you'll only use two or three sentences from me."

After a quick swig, he tried another tack.

"Have you ever met another Serb who knows about Graham Sutherland?" he asked. "And who knows that Turner was the first Impressionist painter?"

"Not yet."

"Well."

He stared at me. We left it at that.

Before we parted, Kapor gave me a signed copy of his historical novel. *Le Tapis Vert du Monténégro*: an account of the Montenegrin struggle for independence against the Turks in the 1870s. On the back cover, there was a short biography of the author.

> Born in Sarajevo, Belgrader by adoption, Momo Kapor is the most popular contemporary Yugoslav writer. He is the author of dozens of works — novels, plays, histories, screenplays and travel books. He is also a well-known painter.

Kapor had worked on the book with a Bosnian artist, Zuko Džumhur. His biography read:

> Descendant of a well known Bosnian family, son of an Imam from Belgrade, [Džumhur] was the most celebrated artist and cartoonist since the Second World War.

Džumhur had died in 1989. I tried to imagine this relationship: the son of an Islamic cleric working with Momo Kapor. But that was then, the late Sixties — before the past came back. A car pulled up outside: Mrs Kapor returning from her tennis match. In the front of his novel, Momo Kapor wrote a slightly ragged inscription:

"To Peter. In order that you might know us better."

A few days after this meeting, I heard about two new organisations which had sprung up in Belgrade. The Association of Old Settlers was a social club for people who had lived in the city for several generations. Even more specific was The Society of True Belgraders. The main qualification for entry was that members — or their parents — should have settled in Belgrade before April 1941, when Nazi troops occupied the city. Of course, the True Belgraders would have hated being seen in the company of Radovan Karadžić or that rude Mr Šešelj; yet their exclusivism ran on the same principle. They, for some reason, were "purer" Serbs: better in some way than the "refugees" whom one saw around the city. "Behind their drawing room manners they still want a Greater Serbia," said one friend. "Only they are the polite devils." Momo Kapor came to Belgrade in 1946.

5　Turbo Folk, Turbo People

Things were coming into focus. Zhirinovsky's aborted rally had offered some insight into the robotic pride of Serb nationalists; Momo Kapor's confessions had added a maudlin, dimly paranoid edge. The politically active Serbs I had met so far seemed to have a rather confused self-image. Their ideas were a volatilé contradiction: a crude sense of superiority coexisted with feelings of vulnerability and doubt. Both traits had been fostered by Serbia's history and culture: the partial legacy, one could say, of an occupied people. Such thoughts had lain dormant in the former Yugoslavia. They had been deliberately revived by Serbia's national leadership in the late 1980s. Slobodan Milošević took a prominent role in engineering these changes. At the rally to celebrate the 600th anniversary of the Battle of Kosovo Polje, Milošević encouraged Serbs to see themselves as a special people. The fact, he added, "that the Serbs are a great people in this region is not a Serbian sin or anything of which to be ashamed. It is, rather, a privilege...the Serbs have never used this privilege even on their own behalf." Milošević's words fused these two traditions: the myths of greatness and of suffering. Serbia, in Milošević's skewed vision, was a superior victim.

The image of immortal Serbia still coloured public opinion. An American academic, Norman Cigar, had monitored this tendency. In his book *Genocide in Bosnia*, he traced the origins of this thinking back through history and theology. Members of the Serbian Orthodox Church legitimised this sense of uniqueness. A Montenegrin cleric declared Serbs to be a "divine" people. "Our destiny is to carry the cross on this blazing divide between [different] worlds," said Metropolitan Amfilohije. "Our people...preserves in its bosom, in its collective memory, Jerusalem's holiness." Such claims often shaded into pathos. Politicians exhibited a strain of *Inat*-style pride when they talked of their nation. "Today, many around the world dream about being Serbs," declared one government minister at the height of

Serbia's hyper-inflation in 1993. "The individual on Fifth Avenue eating a hamburger, the Eskimo breaking the ice and fishing, the Frenchman strolling along the Champs Elysées... Be happy that you are Serbs... Be happy that you belong to this people... You are eternal." At the time, banknotes were being used as toilet paper.

Pride had been fuelled by desperation. Serb nationalism was also governed by a sense of fear, by the perception of Serbia as a nation under threat. Outsiders saw Belgrade as an aggressor, yet Serbs saw themselves as victims of the war rather than its main beneficiaries. History played its functional role. As the first South Slav nation to achieve independence in the nineteenth century, Serbs awarded themselves a special place in the Yugoslav pantheon. "It is not easy to live alongside a people which liberated itself, which has a history of its own," crowed one Serb nationalist in January 1989. "Envy of this is very much a human emotion.... What Serbia did for others, which she is forced to talk about herself, did not arouse gratitude, but stimulated other types of feelings instead." The fact that Bosnia in particular could boast of a distinct, independent existence going back to medieval times was conveniently forgotten.

The threat — as seen through Serb eyes — came from within the borders of former Yugoslavia and from without. One pro-government weekly, *Illustrovana Politika* invited psychiatrist Jovan Striković to speculate on why Serbia was "surrounded by hatred." The good doctor concluded: "Serbia has always been the object and the sweet prize for those who surround it, and I believe that will always be the case, whatever trends civilization takes." Having imagined an enemy, Serbia's political establishment seemed at times unsure about who exactly it was. Slovenes and Croats came within their sights. On other occasions, it was Macedonians. Most of the time however, they fixed on Bosnia's Muslim community.

Serbia's leaders also lashed out at even wilder targets. The Radicals and Momo Kapor had exhibited a marked hostility towards West Europeans and Americans. Newspapers and magazines were clogged with such conspiracies. One pro-Milošević journal, *Duga*, talked of a "Bonn-Vienna-Zagreb-Sofia-Tirana-Rome Axis". Another political commentator assured *Duga's* readers that the Serbs were being attacked as part of the Freemasons' anti-European strategy, designed "to establish an 'Islamic corridor' as a pathway for the breakthrough of Turkish hegemony and of the Islamic masses into Europe."

Pride and paranoia made for a combustible mix. Not all Serbs subscribed to these thoughts — an intelligent minority found them absurd. Yet Serbia's political class, as I already realised, was risibly small. Most people lived in isolated towns and villages. State television and radio provided their main contact with the outside world. Media myths (one TV broadcast spoke of "the blood of a subjugator" flowing in the Bosnian Muslims), combined with folk stories and family traditions to create a powerful current. The nationalists may have expressed these principles in an extreme form, but they were an accepted part of Serbia's political dialogue.

Sociologists and historians have charted this amalgam of self-love and self-loathing in other societies. In *The Roots of Evil: The Origins of Genocide and Other Group Violence*, Erwin Staub explained both these contradictory impulses in terms of man's common desire for security and protection. "A sense of superiority, of being better than others and having the right to rule over them, intensifies this need," he wrote. It also predisposed a group towards violent solutions. The opposite tendency, a feeling of self-doubt can exist at the same time, creating another pressing reason for self-defence. "When a sense of superiority combines with an underlying... self-doubt," wrote Staub, "their contribution to the potential for genocide and mass killing can be especially high."

Such tensions created a moral atmosphere in which extraordinary acts were made possible. They became permissible and excusable.

"At least when operating collectively," wrote sociologist Leo Kuper, "[the perpetrators of genocide] need an ideology to legitimate their behaviour, for without it they would have to see themselves and one another as what they really are — common thieves and murderers."

Equally distressing was the knowledge that these violent urges had been artificially created. They had been grafted onto Serbia (and Croatia) by an inventive political class searching for new excuses to govern. There was nothing "natural" or "inevitable" about the patriotic chants which echoed around Belgrade: someone had fashioned them for a frightened and bewildered people.

So far, I had concentrated on the most obvious traits of Serb nationalism: its childish bluster and wounded swagger. Yet extremists by their very nature can offer only a fraction of the whole picture. I wondered how level-headed Serbs saw the national question. How did "Serbdom" seep into everyday life, and what kind of shared prejudices allowed nationalism to flourish? I recalled a conversation with a Croatian friend in London. Predrag had described how young Yugoslavs learnt about their neighbours. Of course, there were newspapers, books and magazines. But for most children, the most celebrated source of knowledge came from slyly racist jokes. Predrag admitted his first impressions of Albanians from Kosovo had been shaped by playground gags. "It was a form of information," he said, "a way of describing people." As a result, Predrag and his classmates had absorbed all the usual stereotypes about Kosovans before they met anyone from Prishtina or Prizren. The Balkans were a fertile source of humour and folk myths. Jokes were a subtle way of defining a nation (one was either in on the joke, or one was not), and they were an acceptable common currency.

> A Montenegrin soldier is drinking with a Serbian friend. After a few bottles of beer, he starts to boast about his brawling skills.
>
> "One day, I was walking down the street," he says, "when I saw a fight. Three men beating one!"
>
> "What did you do?" asks the Serb.
>
> "Well, I thought about it," the Montenegrin replies. "Should I mix with them or not?"

He pauses to sip his beer.

"So what did you do?" says the Serb. "Did you mix with them or not?"

"Of course I mixed with them," says the Montenegrin.

"And what happened!" hisses the Serb.

"Well," says the Montenegrin proudly, "we beat the shit out of him."

Most of the jokes were in a similar vein: crass or cruel, and usually both. All of them traded on one childish stereotype or another. Montenegrins were vain but brave. The Slovenes were heartless merchants and the Bosnians were rural bumpkins. The gags were not very subtle: many started with that stale construct, "There was a Serb, a Croat and a Slovenian" or some other combination, and descended from there. All the same, I found them fascinating. Behind the polite manners — laid on for visitors along with the best napery — this was how people talked amongst themselves. Jokes revealed how Serbs saw their neighbours and how they regarded themselves. The most unpleasant jokes were told against Croats:

A thunderbolt hits a Croatian house and it begins to burn. The owner panics and starts to move all the furniture out of the house. He jumps in through a window and brings out a TV. Then he leaps in again and drags out a chair. His neighbour is watching from across the garden fence.

"What are you doing?" he shouts. "Your mother-in-law is in there — she'll burn to death!"

"No, no! Don't worry," says the homeowner. "She's fine. She won't burn."

"What do you mean?" asks the horrified neighbour.

The homeowner smiles.

"Well, every time I go in there," he says, "I turn her over."

One could spend several chapters debating the archetypes and nightmares stewing in this gruesome gag. For a start, it confirmed the existence of Balkan mother-in-law jokes. More seriously, this cruel parable helped perpetrate received Serbian wisdom about

Croat behaviour. World War Two had left Serbs with a lingering fear of Croatian brutality: extermination camps formed the core of that terror. The idea of a Croat basting his mother-in-law while a neighbour looks on puts those suspicions into a popular form. When Serbs appeared in their own jokes, it was normally as wise and wily characters. Serbs outwitted their enemies and got the girl (naturally). But urban Serbs also found ways to ridicule their rural brothers. Serb refugees from Krajina had become the latest butt.

> A Serbian soldier from Krajina decides to leave the army.
> "I'm quitting because I'm disgusted with my greedy comrades," he says.
> "What on earth do you mean?" asks his Commander.
> "Well, take my friend for example," says the soldier. "He stole three tractors and seven trailers from those Croats."
> "What's wrong with that?" retorts the Commander.
> "Why the seventh one?" says the soldier. "We all know a tractor can only pull two."

The greatest reserve of jokes though revolved around Bosnia's Muslim population, embodied in the archetypal rural double act of Mujo and Haso. Town-versus-country humour merged here with plain prejudice. I'd heard even politically-correct Yugoslavs making fun of Mujo and Haso. The jokes followed a standard formula: our two chums hatch a plan (to make money, seduce women) and then find their schemes foiled by clever outsiders. Thus a new joke appeared when the United Nations stepped into Bosnia :

> Mujo and Haso spend their evenings with Sarajevo's best prostitutes. They're having a great time until the United Nations troops turn up. The UN soldiers are from western countries, so they've got lots of money. They buy up all the prostitutes and leave Mujo and Haso out on the street — and very frustrated.
> "Look Haso," says Mujo, "before the war we were the screwers. Now we're the ones getting screwed!"

The image of Muslims as eternal victims found a heartless echo in these sketches. At some remote level, they sanctioned the idea that Muslims — drawn here as promiscuous and lazy — somehow deserved their fate, that *this is how they really are*. Jokes helped cement the sense of an "other", of an alien culture. The effect, as Norman Cigar observed in *Genocide in Bosnia*, was to undermine a nation. Jokes about Muslims "reinforced negative images while making light of their victimization.... Negative categorizing can have a devastating effect by dehumanising the target group. It contributes to facilitating their killing as members of an undifferentiated collection of undesirables." In other words, jokes made mass murder easier to tolerate.

Belgrade intellectuals frowned on such insults, but they were shared and embroidered among soldiers on the front line — both Serb and Croat. Such jibes were part of the conditioning of war. As wisecracks helped underwrite the conflict, so in turn conflict eventually killed the joke.

"Twenty years ago, there were lots of colourful jokes about Mujo and Haso," said one friend. "But now there's a crisis of the joke."

"So what happened to Mujo and Haso?" I asked.

"At the start of the Bosnian War, Mujo and Haso met Arkan" (a Serb paramilitary leader).

"And?"

"Well, once Mujo and Haso met Arkan, that really was the end of the story."

Intolerance on this scale had rebounded on Serbs themselves. Anyone with the faintest hint of "Muslim" ancestry was made to stress their "pure" Serb traditions. In one celebrated case, a private banker known as Dafina Milanović felt impelled to deny rumours that her first name was somehow "non-Serbian". In a magazine interview, Dafina pleaded: "Please write, I am not a MUSLIM as recent rumours have it. My name is of Greek origin.... Everyone in my family is a Serb. Anyone who does not believe this should go and see my baptism certificate and those of my parents, as well as our family tree."

Jokes provided a form of mental insulation for Serbia's blockaded people. Turbo Folk imposed the soundtrack, a buttress for the senses. Every war has its distinctive sound and Turbo Folk provided the muzak for this Balkan conflict, irrevocably fixed to its troubled time and place. Belgrade had become a low-rent Nashville: "Neo-Folk" spilled from burger wagons and taxi radios, dank bars and roadside stores. It got everywhere, like the city's stale scent.

Trying to describe Turbo Folk to outsiders, I always struggled to find a clear definition. The foundations were laid by traditional folk music — accordions, doleful strings and throaty ululations — but something new and garish had been built on top, as if a neon display had landed on the thatch of a country cottage. Rap style backbeats and hip-hop samples added the "Turbo" element: ten-foot hair and fish-hook fingernails brought in the glamour. The result was a brittle, chattery form of dance music often souped up with patriotic lyrics. Supporters adopted Turbo Folk as Serbia's "national music", yet it was an oddly hybrid product. The beats were American, the arrangements had an unmistakably Turkish hue. New-style folk was also the sound of isolation: this was what happened when a proud people were closed off by sanctions and then force-fed MTV.

This confusion was loudly in evidence on Serbia's swarm of private TV stations — over 50 in the autumn of 1995 — where Turbo Folk videos were shown in heavy rotation. At first sight, Balkan pop chic had the usual roster of visual tricks. There were candle-struck ruins and smoky chambers, half-hearted vamps and lame jokes. In *Menfolk*, a designer trio called Brena, Vesna and Mira scolded the chaps for their boorish vices — before peeling off their own priestly robes for something rather less Orthodox. In *It's Easy to Die,* the male crooner, Keba, played out a miserable fable. Hunched at a restaurant table, full of *sevdah*, he lamented the loss of his woman, while hugging man's more trusty love — a glass of plum brandy.

In between the girls and the mist, more strident images came out of the screen. A dwarf loped through frame, dressed in the uniform of a Royalist Chetnik from the Second World War. Oil paintings of Serbian kings trotted into view, blessed by crosses. The usable past left its mark here too: national symbols appeared without criticism or irony. Too many people had died for that kind of tone to survive: pop videos aimed to instruct, as well as to entertain. I recalled the words of Milan the economist: these were ways of *whispering* to the population.

Pop music, like almost all private spaces in Serbian life, had been poisoned by nationalism. The realm of music — lyrical thought — had to be occupied and controlled before the real war could begin. Certain meanings were ruled out, while others were crudely drafted in. I watched a popular male singer, Knez, waving a foot-high Orthodox cross around the screen. In American or West European eyes, this would be seen as a sardonic gimmick: the article of faith as designer-prop. In a Serbian context, Knez's cross-wielding display meant he was proud to be a Serb.

Such gestures were echoed on the streets, where the stars of Turbo Folk — the Turbo people — paraded their wealth. Serbs called them *Lovci u mutnom*, or hunters in muddy water. The murk of war provided an ideal cover for this new criminal class: the men sported revolvers and electronic pagers, their peroxide molls flaunted catalogues of jewellery. They came from the fast money fringes of the old society. These were bakers and scrap metal merchants, bar keeps and con artists: entrepreneurs, if you were feeling charitable.

"The women all look like very bad copies of Madonna or Dolly Parton," said Stanimir Ristić , the editor of a traditional folk magazine. "And as the sugar on top, they put a big Orthodox cross on their breast too. So everyone can see that they're very Orthodox. They have no connection with religion, but they know that it is very popular to be Orthodox these days, to show people that you are a real Serb."

Serbs who needed such assurance could get their accessories on Belgrade's main shopping drag, Knez Mihailova — where we'd marched with Vladimir Zhirinovsky. In empty doorways, one found makeshift displays of nationalist kitsch laid out on trestle tables. The sidewalk stalls were less popular than at the height of the Bosnian War in 1993, even though the same lurid trinkets were on sale. Here again were the black woollen hats set off with a *Kokarda*; the car bumper stickers declaring *Ovo je Srbije*: This is Serbia. One found similar totems on the other side of the mirror in Zagreb: Croatian shields and flags lay alongside patriotic cassettes. Like their Croatian counterparts, the Serbian vendors also sold a more venomous musical spin off. Privately made music videos like *Koktel* (Cocktail) contained extremist battle songs from Serbs in Croatia and Bosnia. Most of the video clips had the picture polish of your average wedding video (all trombone zooms and trembling pans), but their sentiments were clear enough. "The Serb is the epitome of pride," chirped Brano Trifković, sitting astride an artillery gun in his camouflage gear. "Be proud to be a Serb in Bosnia." The words were overlaid with pictures of Muslim houses being blown up.

. The shaven head of Bali Mali Knindža appeared. Mali Knindža once turned tunes in German bars. By 1995, he was toasting the Serbian cause. "The Serb isn't afraid of anybody," he crowed from a forest bench. "We'll never be oppressed by anyone, because we're not afraid of anyone." Another singer, Boban Zemunović donned his combat gear to murmur, "Don't give up my Serbia, God is on our side." Zemunović's words, like those of his singing partners, were accompanied by the same plodding beat and wild accordion. There was a certain black twist to watching these interviews in the autumn of 1995, after the Serbs' recent battlefield defeats. The legend of the fearless warrior, as celebrated in the tremulous song, "Chetnik Storm", crumbled somewhat after the Croatian victories.

Perhaps defeat will bring music back to its senses, and Turbo Folk back to its eccentric origins. The term was invented in the late Eighties by one of Yugoslavia's most inventive musicians, the self-styled Rambo Amadeus. Rambo — a Balkan alloy of Frank Zappa and Malcolm McLaren — used "Turbo Folk" to describe music without any clear direction. Rambo thought talk of an exclusively "Serbian" music was nonsense in a region where several cultures overlapped. This was a reason for celebration, in his view, rather than a cause for hysteria.

Calls for a national wartime sound were further undermined by the awkward fact that all sides shared the same songs. In a celebrated broadcast, Radio B92 (the tormentors of Momo Kapor) laid Serbian and Croatian nationalist songs side by side — and found a perfect fit.

Among Serbian soldiers, one antique folk song had been given a fresh coat of patriotic paint:

> *Oh Serbia, Mother do not weep*
> *Struggle fighting, banner fluttering*
> *For the freedom of Serbia!*

Zagreb's wordsmiths had used the same melody for different sentiments:

> *Oh Croatia, Mother do not weep*
> *Struggle fighting, Croatian banner fluttering*
> *For freedom and home, Croatian home!*

By early 1995, the Serbian government was starting to show signs of embarrassment with Turbo-Folk culture. While the war had been going their way in Bosnia, it had been a useful, arm's-length way to exercise control. When the time came to sue for peace, devices were needed to bring people back to normality. For Britons, there was a dark pleasure in learning of the agents chosen for this task. Enter Saatchi and Saatchi, former heralds to the Conservative Party and now hidden persuaders to President Slobodan Milošević. One of the chosen instruments for "the great normalisation" was an arch campaign called "Life is better with Culture." Official posters exhorted weary citizens to visit galleries and concerts — at a time when the most popular form of escapism appeared to be queuing for a visa outside the American embassy. "Life is better with the culture of dialogue!" shouted one display.

After fabricated appeals to "authentic" folk culture, the Serbian experiment had come full circle. For five years, many Serbs had followed the Turbo Folk way of life, in the name of God and Country. All of a sudden, they were told these dreams were wrong. As Saatchi's carefully explained: "Often, a single touch of culture is enough to transform our reality."

6 A Barrel of Stones

I had moved into an edgy world. Serbs saw themselves — in varying degrees — as an elected group, a nation set apart by time and circumstance. People acted differently here. I remembered an old proverb which Dubravka had once used. In Serbia, she said, if one cannot get something nicely, one must grab it roughly. There was a raw edge to the city's street life which conjured both excitement and fear. One afternoon, I spent a cosy hour with a petrol smuggler. He brought his best friend along: a round faced man who turned out to be one of Serbia's leading magistrates. It didn't seem an appropriate time to pursue that handy connection. Our conversation was relaxed and meandering, yet my mind was overwhelmed by a more urgent concern. On arrival, the petrol pirate had removed a small handgun from his waistband and left it nestling by his side, like a mobile phone primed for calls. No one else appeared terribly concerned by this lethal diversion, least of all our learned friend. As for myself, I spent most of that hour sullen with fear. What would happen if the smuggler sat on the trigger, thus sparking a fatal bullet? There were a million sanguinary options. Although I was perched at an oblique angle, a bullet might smite the hotel minibar and then ricochet off the 26 inch telly and into my welcoming skull. At times like that, British etiquette offered no obliging handrail.

Conversely, I realised that Serbs were amused by the relatively buttoned down manner of the British. Most people's mental image of the United Kingdom had been moulded by subtitled swathes of *Monty Python*, *Fawlty Towers* and *Only Fools and Horses*. John Cleese and David Jason were the acme of Britishness as far as most Serbs were concerned. Among younger people, Hugh Grant's bashful toff in *Four Weddings and a Funeral* had become the definitive portrait. But seeing as I wanted to depict Karadžić and Milošević as archetypal Serbs, perhaps I was not in the best position to deride national stereotypes.

Friends in Belgrade laughed even more loudly when they saw their foreign guest acting in a typically "British" manner. When an orange juice failed to appear at the dinner table one night, I asked Dubravka what the problem was. "The problem," she said, in between excited giggles, "is that you didn't ask forcefully enough." My diffident request for the much delayed glass of juice sent her into fresh gulps of laughter. From a Serb perspective, the British obsession with table manners looked neurotic and ludicrously affected. Another friend, Mira, had spent six months working as an au pair in Edgware, North London. "Mealtimes with the English family were terribly funny," she recounted. "If you wanted the salt or the ketchup, you would have to ask someone to pass it down the table. Here, you just snatch it for yourself."

In these asides I learnt more about my own country, and a fair deal about my conditioned responses to Serbia. Visitors are drawn to the most peculiar and extreme parts of an alien culture. One wants to find differences, the points at which countries diverge. By delighting in the manic form of Englishness displayed by Basil Fawlty, Serbs were getting an abbreviated view of my homeland. Yet my own jaunts around Serbia were vulnerable to the same criticisms. Was I getting an accurate picture of the country as a whole, I wondered, or merely an excitable reflection of my own prejudices?

Serbia was still palpably different, undeniably *other*. Reading an art magazine one afternoon, I came across an essay by Katarina Pejović. Much of her article was devoted to exploring the Serbian tradition of *Vrlo Grube Vitalnosti*: the principle of rough vitality. It was a cherishable phrase, and one which she explored with an intriguing parable about the Serbs and the Brits.

At the end of the last century, a Belgrade merchant approached a London fruit wholesaler with an inventive plan to sell Serbian plums on the British market. The trader's argument was simple: Serbian plum jam would be an exotic addition to the jaded Victorian breakfast table. Our London dealer agreed, and paid in advance for his first consignment.

A few weeks later, a barrel arrived in London. Hurrying back to his warehouse, the wholesaler took the lid off his new purchase and let out a cry of anger. Beneath a thin layer of plums, the wooden container was filled with pebbles of various shapes and sizes. The British merchant had been conned into buying a barrel of stones. "What the English will never understand," wrote Ms Pejović, "is that this method not only lives on in these parts, but that the descendants of that ingenious peasant have brought it to perfection and built an entire Empire on it."

A Barrel of Stones. The sentence held a kind of poetry, an imagined truth not just about Victorian traders but about Serbia and its people. The incident no doubt confirmed British perceptions of Balkan duplicity, a tradition which continues to the present day. But Ms Pejović suggested that something more valuable than money had been lost in this thwarted transaction. "The English were thus introduced to a specific way of trading," she chuckled. "[But] gourmets from the island were forever deprived of getting to know the taste of Serbian plums."

Even more absorbing, the author claimed that this notorious Barrel of Stones still existed. Ms Pejović assured the astonished reader that it was on permanent display at what she called "The Museum of Trade in London". The name was not familiar: something must have got lost in translation. I imagined the barrel was probably exhibited at the Victoria and Albert Museum or the Museum of London, along with a thousand other examples of colonial swag. I wondered how the real barrel would measure up to my own collection of Serbian plums and stones. Here was something to track down when I returned to London.

The crafty cask was a symbol of past misunderstandings. There were plenty of other signs and portents which I didn't quite get. Every day there were reminders that I was living in a warped, wartime barrel. Take road signs. We were on the road to Šabać when I started to notice the problem. At a literal level, they were clear enough: high metal panels with brisk tips on distance and direction. As factual guides though, they were close to useless. Every few miles, the bold blue and yellow rectangles would offer directions to Sarajevo and Zagreb: cities which once belonged to the same country. For the moment, they appeared part of a separate continent.

That day, I was on a bus heading west. Sunlight caught the dusty seats and made them warm. Fields of pale grass ran past the window and October was in the ochre leaves. The signposts had turned into roadside memorials, unwitting tributes to the old Yugoslavia. There were no direct road or telephone links between the three capitals at this time. Without these means to create a shared present, the Bosnian and Croatian capitals had ceased to exist for Serbs. They had become as one dimensional as the road signs which recalled them. Without a common present, there was more room for separate pasts, for separate orbits. That mental parting had made the defilement of one capital and the demonisation of another easier for Serbs to accept. Srebrenica was so small it did not merit a signpost. North to Tuzla or west to Mostar: the road signs promised imaginary trips to impossible places. Some of the most banal actions had become the most incredible.

I was lost. I needed a map. Yet former Yugoslavia was one place where maps and charts left the visitor more confused rather than less. Each diagram presented only a partial vision, an economical take on the truth.

My first encounter came in Banja Luka. It was early in the war, autumn 1992.

The spelling mistake was appropriate in a bleak kind of way. Behind Major Milutinović's desk there hung a large map of Bosnia. The country had been shaded into ripples of blue, green and red to represent the republic's three national groups: Croat, Bosnian and Serb respectively. Red was the dominant colour. From a distance, the map looked like a bruise, a mugger's kiss inflicted on some innocent body. Beneath the diagram, a tilting title had been stencilled onto the page: "Ethical Division of Bosnia-Hercegovina, April 1992."

Major Milutinović had not corrected the spelling error. Perhaps in his view, ethics and ethnics were interchangeable.

"Everyone knows Serbs are the real moral victors of this war," he said. "There is absolutely no question about that."

The Major took a fresh draw on his Drina cigarette, and winced. People only smoked Drinas — appropriately named after the toxic river which bisected Serbia and Bosnia — when they ran out of black-market Marlboros. Lighting up a stale Drina seemed the highest act of Bosnian Serb patriotism, equal in combat prestige to a stint on the front line.

We nodded and smiled. Major Milutinović ran the self-styled "International Press Bureau" at Banja Luka, northern outpost of the self-styled *Republika Srpska*, the Serb Republic gouged out of the former Federal Republic of Bosnia Hercegovina. It was October 1992, and our film crew had come to the headquarters of the Serbian First Krajina Corps for an interview with the Bosnian Serb Army Commander, General Ratko Mladić. We had reached Banja Luka after a nervy two-day journey along the corridor which links Serb-controlled Bosnia to Serbia proper.

The Major looked like he spent most mornings getting over the night before: all saggy eyed and sour. While we waited, he offered us a pamphlet printed on thin paper and written almost entirely in capital letters, like graffiti. "THE SERBS WANTED TO PRESERVE THE FEDERATION AND WERE OPPOSED TO THE LEBANISATION (sic) OF YUGOSLAVIA," it shouted. Another tract was called "THE TRUTH IS COMPLETELY DIFFERENT."

I returned to the map. Each council district had been overlaid with complex pie charts and bar graphs, showing Serbian majorities across the republic. It had been drafted to help fight the war; there was no way of telling how accurate the figures were or whether they still reflected any kind of reality. Given the circumstances, this was rather an abstract point: Serbs believed the half truths contained in the map and that was all that mattered as far as Major Milutinović was concerned.

We flipped through the Major's tracts and tried some polite remarks, then turned to the object of our visit. Major Milutinović smiled and shrugged his khaki shoulders.

"I'm sorry, but General Mladić isn't here," he said, without much evident regret. "We don't know where the General is. He left Banja Luka yesterday for the front lines."

Two years later, I looked at the same country from the opposite point of view.

The British Army map had a rather drab title : "HQ BRITFOR — Current Situation Map, as at 30 May 1994." Just below the heading, a curt sentence had been added in red capitals: "FOR OFFICIAL USE ONLY." To be on the safe side, the warning was repeated at the bottom of the A3 page, next to a short note. "This map," it said, "is not to be taken as necessarily representing the views of the UN on boundaries or political status."

Ignoring these mental bye-laws, I scanned the chart. As one would expect from a people obsessed with sun and rain, the British had turned Bosnia into a weather map. Front lines appeared as thin isobars, linking towns under high pressure; advances were marked with the kind of cartoon arrows normally used for wind speeds over the North Sea. Compared to the local maps, this British version of Bosnia felt snugly familiar, a kind of Little England. Its signs and symbols had been adapted from Ordnance Survey maps; all that was missing were a few historic churches and bridle ways for the weekend rambler.

But the more I looked at the map, the less I could see. By accident rather than intention, most of Yugoslavia's towns and cities had disappeared under an alien tracery of aid routes and supply depots. A new kind of country came through the page, divided into United Nations "zones" and "sectors". Places like Zenica and Drvar were obscured, as if viewed through several panes of thick glass. This was another Bosnia: a territory reshaped and customised for the needs of outsiders. The Brits had even renamed some of the roads. Some of their names had a rough beauty: the busiest supply route along the Adriatic Coast was dubbed Gannet. Central Bosnia was fed along the robust sounding Route Diamond. Further north, a more ironic streak was evident on the roads leading to Doboj and Gradacac. Aid convoys found it hard to reach these contested towns. On the occasions when they did manage to get through, most of their supplies were creamed off by local soldiers. The British had christened these roads Lada and Skoda.

Back in Belgrade in the autumn of 1995, I picked up a copy of trusty *Politika*. Tired of struggling with a Cyrillic run down of that day's TV programmes, my eyes wandered to the weather maps at the bottom of the back page. According to the forecasters at *Politika*, London and Paris were due some late sun, while Moscow was set for heavy rain. The regional weather map was rather more interesting. Serb-held Krajina had fallen to Croat forces three months earlier, yet the weather chart still showed the area as Serb-controlled. *Politika* was predicting a sunny day for Krajina, even though there were few Serbs left there to appreciate it. The map of Bosnia was equally detached from reality: according to *Politika*, Serbs still enjoyed two thirds of the Bosnian weather. In truth, it should have been nearer to one half.

Over the next few days, I asked people why the weather map had not adjusted to the new military climate.

One friend took the *Javašluk* position.

"It's just laziness," he suggested. "The designers can't be bothered to make a new one."

An academic was more inventive.

"They don't want to alter the map in case it upsets refugees from Krajina," she said. "By keeping the old one, it encourages them to think they might return."

The nationalist shook his head.

"That's not a map of the past you know," he grunted. "That's a map of Serbia in the future."

The liberal gave a sly smile.

"The map will only change when Milošević's wife, Mira Marković, says so," he said. "And when that back page map changes, that really will be front page news. Because it will signal that the Greater Serbian dream is over."

That sounded more like the truth, or a Serbian version of the truth. One found the reliable news in weather maps and horoscopes. Real exclusives appeared on the back page rather than the front. I was still lost, although I had a better sense of where I was.

My final exercise came one October afternoon.

The taxi driver checked his map. We were in the right place, he said. This was definitely Tolstoyeva Street, this was the house we wanted. I was looking for the Soros Foundation and yet our building didn't look very charitable: an empty mansion with a brace of BMWs at the door. None of the cars had registration plates. Mind you, Dedinje was full of houses like that. This was Belgrade's secret suburb: a woody maze of official houses and illicit palaces. Milošević lived there too. I walked up the drive. There was no one around so I pushed the white front door: newspapers on the floor, a lightbulb flaring in the basement. Silence. An impression of sudden departure. On the right, an empty reception room coated with chocolate brown wallpaper. In the middle of the bare floor I could see the shadow of a settee.

Without warning, a man jumped up from the other side of the sofa. He wore a light blue track top and jeans, a beer bottle in his hand.

"Is this the Soros Foundation?" I asked lamely.

He frowned.

"No, it's not. Who are you?"

A second man, dressed in Militia gear, entered the room. He had a gun belt. This raised the odds somewhat.

"I'm looking for the Soros Foundation," I said, hoping to gain some time. The militia man looked me over.

"You need the next street," he said. "Why are you here?"

"I'm sorry. It's been a mistake." All I could think was: keep calm, don't show them your press card. I raised my palms in mock surrender: the dozy foreigner act. After a few more seconds of slow thought, the militia man nodded — a sign that I should leave. Track top man came to the front door and watched me walk down the drive. I had been in the house for less than a minute.

Later, I told Florida Dragan about what had happened.

"You probably walked into a house being used by the Bosnian Serb leaders," he said. "It's not a good idea to go up there."

Even in Belgrade, one could not escape the war. Each night there were shooting incidents in town. Military helicopters swept across the city. Where was the front line? You could not find it on maps. It was everywhere.

7 Milošević — The Early Years

We met once. He probably doesn't remember the occasion. After all, it was several peace treaties ago. We were in a snow crusted car park in Kragujevac, southern Serbia — a dynamite factory, apparently — in December 1993. The Serbian President was working the crowd as part of his re-election campaign. All around us, people clapped and whooped as if he had already won. But then as a former Communist, Milošević believed one should never hold an election unless one could be sure of the result. We had been stalking him all morning in the hope of a short TV interview: a "doorstep" in media shorthand. Our efforts though were failing on two fronts. Shaven heavies blocked our camera-man's view, and in the rare moments when Milošević was in earshot, he seemed to lose the power of hearing. Like most politicians, our quarry had acquired Selective Ear Syndrome: the ability to hear a lisping octogenarian voter at twenty paces while apparently unaware of the journalist shouting "When will you resign?" from two feet away.

Milošević wouldn't talk, but we had a chance to stare. I had seen the Serbian President on television many times and there was a queasy fascination in watching him perform in real life: the despot in the dark blue raincoat. His hair shot upwards in white receding tufts like spring shoots. As for the famous ears, they were impressively large. The taut lips hinted at a harsher interior, as did the stiff gestures he was performing for his audience. Milošević's jutting chin and distant eyes suggested higher concerns: the square head turned upwards as if breasting an unpleasant smell. I watched the handshake and the walk. Everything was clipped and contained. I imagined a man with a shattering temper: when he spoke, his mouth hardly moved.

For some reason, Milošević decided the dynamite factory car park was a good place for a press conference. TV Serbia leapt in with a few underarm pitches ("Mr President, what does Serbia most need today?"), followed by some relative hardballs from Radio Kragujevac ("Mr President, why is Serbia suffering under these unjust and unwarranted sanctions?"). While the bodyguards looked away, our reporter dived in. Milošević was still and solitary. He looked surprised, which was odd seeing as we had tried to trip him up at least five times that day. Time was short, so the conversation went something like this:

> *Reporter:* President Milošević! How's the campaign going?
> *Milošević: (warily)* What campaign?
> *Reporter:* You know, the one for the election?
> *Milošević (nodding):* Uh. Ah — that campaign. *(Pause)* Yes. We have no problems with our campaign. Thank you! *(He laughs and walks away)*

That was as close as I ever got to Milošević, and I'm still not clear whether the joke was slyly intentional. The nearest most civilians got to their President was through a bland looking column in the magazine *Duga*. Every fortnight, President Milošević's wife Mira Marković wrote what she called a "creative interpretation" of events in an open diary. Journalists scrutinised her words as closely as the Politburo line up in old May Day parades. Cynics remarked on her staggering gift for political clairvoyance: no sooner had Mira said something, then it started to happen. Just before the 1992 elections, Mrs Milošević declared: "This is not a time for the centre. This is the season for the aggressive and the radical." A few weeks later, Vojislav Šešelj's Radical Party became the second largest party in the Serbian Parliament. Conversely, a minxish diary entry from Mira Marković was enough to hole any political career — as Šešelj himself found out a year later.

Some of the whispering was more dogmatic. Mira Marković's column contained some classic examples of political double think. There was a striking wish to blame others for the conflict. According to the leader's wife, the war had been plotted by "fifth columnists" intent on bringing "Yugoslavia" to its knees. "Of all the bullets fired throughout [Europe's] history, most have been aimed at Balkan hearts," she wrote. Yugoslavia's other republics started the drift to war, she claimed. In this world, Mira's husband was merely a concerned observer.

Diplomats read the column too: it was one way to find out what was going on. One foreign envoy ("No names or countries please") had watched the Miloševićs at work for several years. We talked in his office, a dark panelled room the size of a squash court. The diplomat's assessment was blunt, matter of fact. Slobodan Milošević was "very straightforward. No baggage, you know." His wife was "very dogmatic, very doctrinaire."

His strongest criticisms though were reserved for the other Balkan leaders.

"As for Tudjman [the Croat President]...." He paused. "Well, Tudjman is, ah... Tudjman. And the Bosnians, we're never quite sure who's in charge there. I mean, we'll agree something with Izetbegović [the Bosnian President] and then Silajdzić [the then Prime Minister] will turn up and everything's changed."

So that was how the diplomats saw it. Milošević broke his promises like the other Balkan Presidents. It was just that he broke them more professionally. To steal a phrase, he was a man they could do business with.

Milošević was a conundrum. Amateur psychologists pointed to his traumatic family background: strong willed parents who both committed suicide. Others looked to Mira Marković, dubbed "Lady Macbeth" by Belgrade's transfixed press corps. Opposition journalists wrote about the leader with a mixture of contempt and weary admiration. Writing in the summer of 1993, Alexander Vasović conceded that in the short term, "he's a phenomenal operator and always two steps ahead of his political opponents... He always has at least two or three aces, plans and subplans up his sleeve." Two years later, Miloš Vasić was equally direct. Milošević's ambition, he wrote, "is to remain in power as long as possible.... He is a slow player and he seldom strikes before thorough preparations."

I got another view from a retired liberal politician, whom I'll call Borislav. I went round to see Borislav at his house in old Belgrade. We sipped Earl Grey tea and German orange juice as he recalled Milošević's early years. Hardback books of history and philosophy filled one wall. A former academic, Borislav had watched Milošević from close quarters, as a former political rival.

"You must realise that Milošević is a product of two forces," he began. "The Army and the nationalists. The question is — who is using who?"

Borislav laughed.

"He's like Stalin in some respects you know. He enjoys power, and he's always been underestimated. At first he was called 'Little Slobo', and the party bosses looked after him. He got the organisation jobs, just like Stalin. He was always there."

"What's he like?" I asked.

"The only thing he sincerely likes is the Communist Party," said Borislav. "He never learned to say 'Mister' instead of 'Comrade'. I was teaching at the university when Milošević was a law student there in the early Sixties. He was timid then, not so self-assured. He took over as student party secretary, and spent all day in their special office. At eight o'clock every night, the office would be closed, but Milošević would always hang around. All the other guys would be out chasing girls, but he'd still be there, walking around the corridors. He always looked desperately lost when the office was shut. He had this big leather satchel in one hand, and he just stood there, looking around. He had nowhere to go. He didn't know what to do."

Politics gave Milošević an occupation. At the Eighth Party Congress in 1987, he committed an act of political parricide — deposing his former mentor, Ivan Stambolić as leader of the Serbian Communists.

"Everybody fell in love with Milošević in 1987," Borislav went on. "But the saddest thing was there were hardly any political jokes about him for three or four years. He doesn't try to woo the population: he doesn't like them all that much. He talks to them with the same 500 words, the same reduced language. You know, 'Serbs are reasonable, they want to live together, blah blah blah'."

I'd heard one story about Milošević, so I shared it with

Borislav. A man went round to Milošević's family house in Požarevac, south of Belgrade. As he sat down at the dining table, a hand gun slipped out of his jacket, falling on the floor. Milošević frowned. "Dear friend," he said in his husky drone, "I will not allow guns in my house. Why do you bring such a weapon in here?" The man shrugged his shoulders. "Because the last time I handed my gun over to your security men," he said, "they stole all my bullets."

Borislav chuckled. Which was polite of him really, as he'd heard the story before.

"The thing about Milošević," he went on, "is that he's surrounded himself with people of proven inability. They're no threat to him, you see. They're very obedient.

"Another thing people don't realise is that he's got a very dirty mouth. He's always using expletives. In Serbian, there's a pretty foul expression which means we don't give a damn. You know, 'Such and such a thing doesn't bother me — even though it burns my ass'. Milošević is even cruder. He changes the end of that phrase so it means 'Even though it burns my prick'. He acts it out too. That helps bring the point home."

I tried to imagine it. And then I recalled the student politician, lost in the evening corridors.

"Tudjman, the Croatian President, is like Tito. He's slightly comical — all the uniforms, colourful parades. Milošević though, he's another kind of character. He hates all that stuff — the flowers, greeting children. The most dangerous dictators are the ascetic ones."

Borislav emptied his tea cup. He had guessed my last question. "Why did we get Milošević? There was some kind of emptiness here, a lack of expressive identity. There was a vacuum that he filled, that's all."

8 Živorad's Version

Perica worked from a set of rooms at Yugoslav Army Headquarters. His offices were midway down a neglected corridor, a short cut to somewhere else. Lime green paint blistered away on the walls; the carpet looked and smelt like stale gravy. I was surprised to find Perica here. In theory, there was no longer any connection between the Yugoslav People's Army, the JNA, and the Bosnian war. President Milošević always insisted on that point. In Geneva and Paris, London and Moscow, the President repeated his catechism. The Bosnian conflict was a civil war between three groups he said: Serbia proper had no say over the outcome.

So it was odd, to say the least, to find the Association of Bosnian War Veterans tucked away in a rank corner of JNA HQ, Belgrade. A military journalist had suggested I pay them a visit. The Association looked after men and women who had fought in Croatia and Bosnia. The journalist hinted that it was also a contact point for new recruits. Some of the soldiers who had rampaged around Srebrenica may have passed through these secret passages. Having spent time with the ideologues of Serb nationalism, I wanted to meet the regular soldiers. I wondered how the conflict appeared through their eyes. What kind of threats, both real and imagined, turned a man — and it was mostly men, of course — to violence? After almost fifty years of reasonable co-existence, what strain of primary fury drove a man to murder his neighbour or even his brother in law. The nearest I had come to this mentality in the past had been on brief visits to Northern Ireland. In nationalist and loyalist parts of the country, political murder was justified in eternally simple terms. Survival was the key. Kill your enemies before they kill you. Murder became an absorbing race, where both sides tried to get their retaliation in first.

The Veterans' office was behind a large white door. Harsh laughter seeped into the corridor, an anecdote in mid-flow. I knocked on the heavy wood. After a series of clicks and rattles, an inner door was unlocked and a bolt pulled on the outer entrance. A crop-haired man with a thick moustache peered round the doorframe, checking out the visitor. His eyes lurched around, searching for bombs or pistol bulges. He reminded me of the gun-glazed kids who ran checkpoints across Bosnia: the kind of folk who fired off guns before questions. Satisfied I was not an Islamic Fundamentalist or some other imagined enemy, the doorman let me in.

Perica was a short man with a firm handshake. He walked with a slight limp. I naturally assumed this to be a legacy of the war: some dramatic wound from the Bosnian frontlines. This was the first of several wrong assumptions on my part. Perica later disclosed that his leg had been badly broken in a car accident ten years earlier. I decided to believe him, for there was no immediate way of checking the story.

Perica's fleshy features and narrow eyes reminded me of the Bosnian Serb Army Commander, Ratko Mladić. Perica was younger though: a dour man in his thirties. There was no sign of the loud humour which had leaked under the comrades' door. A foreigner had broken into their small circle and there was no desire to make him feel at home. Faced by three soldiers in an obscure office, I felt a long way from home.

In his black bomber jacket and matching combat trousers, Perica looked like a bouncer on his tea break. After a nod to his colleagues, he guided me into his inner office: a large, sky-blue room equipped with a desk and two stools. A wooden wheelchair was parked in the corner. Judging by its weathered joints, the chair had seen service in several earlier wars and would no doubt oblige again in the future. The sight brought back one visit to a makeshift Croatian mortuary near Vitez, Central Bosnia. It was a Sunday morning in early summer, a sharp light held up to our day. Inside the building, the air was soured with shit and disinfectant. We held our breath and our thoughts. For fifteen minutes or so, our camera team walked from one room to another, filming corpses as if this was a perfectly normal thing to do on a Sunday. Small details stayed in my mind: a pair of waxed feet poking out from a muddy shroud; the dirt-packed fingernails on a teenager's hand, his final home in the earthy trenches. Death was overwhelming. Walking outside for air, I came across another dismal exhibit, all the more affecting for being unexpected. A brown and orange sun bed was propped up against a pebbledash wall, its flowery motifs mottled with old blood. The sun bed had become a makeshift stretcher, sent out on midnight tours of the front lines. And I thought of the summers it had seen, of clipped lawns and childish children; of how the careless sun continued to warm the cloth.

"I went to war for the security of my family," said Perica. "I joined the Serb Army of Krajina in August 1991. We formed little groups and fought in the forest against the Croatian police."

His voice was deep and precise, the answers delivered with leaden certainty. I asked how he had come to join the army. Was there one incident which had made a difference?

"I was watching the TV every night and I could see the work of the Croatian Ustaša there. I said to my wife: 'I must go and fight'."

"What did your wife make of that?"

Perica paused. There was one point I had to understand, he said. He was talking about family history, of an inherited memory.

"In the Second World War, the Ustaša killed my mother's parents. And then my mother spent a year in a camp at Nova Gradiska — and she said to me all the time, 'The Ustaša are not good. They are killers, wrong men'."

He smiled.

"Of course, I still have friends in Zagreb. That was normal in the old Yugoslavia, but not any more. I mean, I have friends there though I haven't spoken to them for five years because the telephone lines have been cut."

"Do you know if they're okay?"

"I watch the TV news to see if any of my friends are in the Croatian Army. I don't think anything of it. I mean, they're dying for their country too. I have my nation, they have theirs. I go to war for my people. They go for theirs. That's no problem to me."

Perica had turned the war into a series of neat, self-contained equations. Perhaps that was how he managed to live with its cruelty. I sensed that an older, larger part of himself had been denied.

Perica did not see the conflict as a moral question where Serbs had to consider their share of the blame. This was not an open debate. Matters were closed and definite. Family history had also left a powerful impress, making Perica more open to stories of Croatian atrocities. He was living in Ivan Čolović's two temporal dimensions: existing in the present and in some mythical "historic" time where war offered the chance to avenge his ancestors. Television was his friend and guide, a constant source of reference.

"What was your job in the war," I asked.

Perica laughed.

"I was a soldier."

"What kind of soldier? Where did you fight?"

"I fought in Krajina and Sarajevo. I was not skilled with a machine gun."

Something in Perica's words and manner made this sound like false modesty. He was harsh and distant: there was no intent to charm. Here was someone who knew one end of a Kalashnikov from another. I sensed that my host would not have refused his wartime tasks. My next question was absurdly blunt, but seemed the only way to gain an open response.

"Have you killed anyone?" I said.

Perica stared at the desk for several moments. Outside, traffic burred. I examined the wooden wheelchair.

"Yes. I shot people. Maybe I killed them. Maybe not. War is war. People go to war for killing, not for flowers."

Perica saw me frown and corrected himself. Slightly.

"You know, many people who go to war don't think badly of other people. They go to war only for their own people, for my people. Good men go in for their own people. There's no hatred of the other side."

I wondered whether such thoughts made killing easier. Did they help tighten the finger on the trigger? Murder in Perica's mind was the logical side effect of defending one's people, a necessary act of self-protection. The question was how far he was ready to take this principle. At a contained level, it fitted within the same desperate frame as Northern Ireland. As long as we report the victims' names said one Irish journalist, then the deaths will not be in vain. But how could one describe the mass killings which possessed Bosnia, where individual names were lost in a haze of overpowering figures?

Srebrenica came into that category: the stage at which an irrational fear degenerates into extermination. I thought of the rows of Muslim men, of the bloodied shirt; that was the end of restraint, of all humane controls.

"When did you stop fighting," I asked.

"November 1993. In Hercegovina. I had to stop."

"Why?"

Perica examined his large hands.

"I saw many things in this war and I decided to stop. I have a family. I have a wife."

"What did you see?"

"Things. I feel a small shame now because I am not in Bosnia you know. I sit here and worry about my friends. It's not good. Men in war are my brothers. All my friends in this war were very strong men, crazy men. They didn't have fear."

When Perica talked about his personal feelings like this, the burly words seemed to skim his real thoughts. He did not want to examine his heart too closely. He was more animated on the mechanics of battle, so we talked about his favourite campaign: the battle for Sarajevo. My attention wandered to a calendar nailed to the door. It had been sponsored by a military magazine called *Serbian Army*. October showed General Ratko Mladić set against a ski lift and a snowy hillside. The General had been snapped in a heroic, NATO-defying pose: chin turned upwards against Serbia's many enemies. A pair of khaki-green binoculars were strung around his thick neck. Some people found this inspiring.

As a final question, I wanted to know what Perica had done before the war. Was there a job he could go back to when the fighting was over?

"Before all this I was a dancing master," he said. "Folk dancing was my speciality, along with a little ballet. Before the war, I used to dance in Zagreb. I taught students all about dance. There was a dance group in the city as well. I used to enjoy that."

A dancing master. I had not imagined such a history. Warriors were meant to have illicit pasts, but then I had probably seen too many movies. I saw Perica as a loutish bar tender or some small-town salesman. This made it even more difficult to square past and present. On the other hand, I could also see how Perica had been enticed to war. His family past almost determined the outcome, once the wider conflict was declared. His attachment to folk dancing also reflected an interest in tradition: it was another rite to be upheld. In Perica's mind, these were totems worth defending. For the first time, I put myself in his position. Were there any aspects of my own life that were worth protecting to the death? I was grateful for being denied that kind of choice.

Perica walked me to the door. His colleagues grunted a farewell. Before parting, he named a military hospital near the Bosnian border where I might find some veterans. Sure, there were soldiers in Belgrade he admitted, but it would be difficult to find them. Anyway, the office was always busy. It was enough of a hint. Perica shook my hand again with the same low level warmth, and closed the double doors behind him.

There were all kinds of soldiers in Bosnia. Few of them knew how to fight. There were mercenaries and conscripts, fanatics and thieves. One greedy breed of Serbian fighters were dubbed the weekenders: on Friday nights they would travel into Bosnia for a lost weekend of dedicated pillaging, returning home on Sunday night with bootfuls of consumer durables. At the top of the military tree were career officers like Ratko Mladić. Trained in the Yugoslav Army, they ran the war in a shockingly efficient manner. To begin with, the Serbs' military strategy was brutal but effective. Ring a town with artillery guns and then shell its people to the edge of insanity. That was General Mladić's plan for Sarajevo. Later, the tactic was extended to the east Bosnian towns

of Žepa, Goražde and Srebrenica. It was only reversed when
NATO finally decided to pitch its greater firepower into the mix.
That, and a stronger Croatian army helped to restore a kind of
balance.

Viewed from a distance — or through the obliging filter of a
camera lens — the conflict presented itself as a series of random
atrocities. Now and then, one needed to recall that this had all
been planned: someone had wanted these events to happen at a
certain time and in a certain order. There was a design. Zoran
Petrović's video from Srebrenica was proof of that. He had filmed
buses parked in dusty ditches, soldiers with bandoleers training
their pistols at the grass.

By 1995, Croatia's army in Bosnia was equally well supplied
and staffed. A day trip to Croat headquarters in the Hercegovinan
town of Grude offered ample confirmation: black Mercedes and
BMWs coursed the streets and alleys, their passengers burdened
with military brass. As for the Bosnian Government side, they
began the war at a severe disadvantage. Desperately short of guns
and heavy weapons, they relied on erratic hand-me-downs from
old Yugoslav Army bases. In July 1993, we took a tour around
the front lines of Bihać. Bosnian Government troops faced Serb
forces on three sides. Jealous of my own safety, I kept the flak
jacket and helmet firmly strapped on during our three-hour visit.
The Bosnian soldiers had no such protection. As if we needed
reminding, this was a conflict between three unevenly matched
armies. At rest in their shallow trench, the Bosnian fighters wore
turquoise T-shirts and tracksuit trousers. One soldier showed us
a scruffy rifle with 1948 stamped on its butt.

I was interested in these kind of soldiers, largely because they
were not soldiers at all. We found the same kinds of people on
every frontline. They were carpenters and teachers, shopkeepers
and car mechanics. Most had been dragged into the war, donning
their "national identity" as reluctantly as their uniforms. Others
took to their new vocation with gusto. In Vitez, we heard of one
Croatian mortar expert who maintained his peace-time job as a
postman. After emptying his thin mailbag around Upper Vitez,
the soldier would retire to his back garden and fire mortars at this

week's enemy. The British media called him Postman Splat.

Some of these tyro soldiers loved their new calling. They had found their place in time, a sense of excitement denied in peace. Young men with marginal lives and zero prospects had no stake in normality. War offered them a chance for quick distinction. I could not see the attraction, but then I had not tasted their kind of despair either. Perica understood. The war had given him and many others a rude stage on which to shine. Perica knew there were no rational explanations for this, and he had mocked my attempts to find any. Why did people erase friends and families, destroy their neighbours' homes and possessions? These were matters of emotion and instinct, beneath (or above) debate and reason.

Banja Koviljaća was a good place for a geography lesson. While carts and mopeds stuttered by, I tried to get my bearings. I was on the outer edge of Serbia, at its natural glistening end on the River Drina. Further west, Bosnia's disputed ranges lined the morning sky. The Majevica hills started around Brćko and Tuzla in the north and gained their southern tip around Zvornik, ten miles from where I was standing. To my unknowing gaze, distance turned these hills into tempting shapes, whorls of muted green and brown. Soldiers saw them another way: as land to be captured and controlled. I was still in Serbia proper, though Bosnia and its war were within walking distance. Each car seemed to carry a platoon of soldiers, smoking energetically behind crazed windscreens. Roadside cafes were thick with men in uniform, killing their day. From each entrance, there was the rhythmic thunk thunk of Turbo Folk. Dressed in a fawn raincoat and jeans, I felt more conspicuous here than on Belgrade's plural streets. Keen to fit in, I wandered into a store selling motor parts. A policeman gave me a long look and whispered into his radio. Time to move on.

We were near to Bosnia and by the same reasoning, Bosnia and its nasty conflict were near to us. The last time I had visited Banja Koviljaća in June 1993, we had to tread warily. A few days earlier, a stray shell had landed outside a house, killing one elderly woman. People blamed Bosnian Government troops just across the border, though one could never be sure. Serbian mortars sometimes went the wrong way. The story was mournfully relayed by a barman. "Where did it happen?" we demanded, eager for incident. "About ten metres from here," he said. "Across the road."

Three days before my present journey, another missile had dropped on the town. This time the mortar had failed to explode, having lodged in a backyard vegetable patch. Olja the interpreter said it was the talk of the town. "This is the first attack since that lady was killed two years ago," she said. That coincidence cheered me up, particularly as the second mortar had landed close to the object of my visit: a sanatorium in the wooded hills above Banja Koviljača. Perica had directed me here.

We approached the complex along a damp forest path. The sanatorium revealed itself through flickering branches. A gloomy mansion, it looked like a seedy cousin to the Von Trapp family's residence in *The Sound of Music*. The towers and lengthy wings were turned in white and grey. This was the kind of place which looked better at night, largely because one could avoid its heavy attentions. Mortars were still on my mind even though the only actual danger came from a slow lode of drizzle.

Inside, there was an air of endemic misery. We climbed a dank stairway to the Director's office. On each floor, men sat by windows. One elderly patient patrolled his landing in a squeaky wheelchair. Beneath the knotted sash of his purple dressing gown, a cream blanket hid his abbreviated body. Living with such injuries was hard enough, but the conditions at Banja Koviljača added an extra taint of humiliation. Like the dead, these injured men were kept away from the visible world. People did not want to be reminded of them.

The Director, Milena Jovanović, welcomed us to her shadowy rest room and made several cups of coffee. Mrs Jovanović was short and broad, and sighed frequently. "We are in a bad situation," she said over a cigarette. "Sanctions mean that our medicines are out of date. Some of our bandages are from 1944. They were left here in Yugoslavia by the US Army."

Mrs Jovanović took us to a small ward at the sheltered rear of the building. Mortars worried her too. There were eight beds in the room, all filled by men in their forties and fifties. We entered to a ripple of groans and coughs. Heads turned slowly towards the door. More by luck than judgement, the first patient we spoke to had fought near Srebrenica. Živorad Radić was a small, pale man with an ample moustache. I could imagine Živorad in a uniform: his plastic features seemed to seek a sharper definition. Under a pair of blue and white pyjamas, his left leg was frozen in thick plaster. Healing time clearly passed heavily for Živorad. A carton of sunny fruit juice stood on his bedside table along with a plastic beaker. There were no books or papers in sight. I asked about the injury.

"We were in Baljkovica last July, a place between Tuzla and Zvornik," he said. "While our boys were attacking Srebrenica, the Muslims launched an offensive at us. There were about 250 of them with weapons. I went to see what was happening, and well..."

Živorad examined his leg.

"A machine gun did that," he said mildly, as if referring to a chip in the family dining table. One could present this as courage or stupidity: two qualities which often blurred into each other on military adventures.

"My family is from Zvornik," he said. "But I was an electrician in Belgrade. I worked there for 22 years."

This was a familiar story. Many Bosnians had moved to larger towns and cities in Yugoslavia, looking for better opportunities. Urban life often widened people's perspectives and moderated their political prejudices. In short, city life made folk more tolerant. Živorad was not one of them.

"I fought in the Bosnian Serb Army from the start of the war," he said, a twitch of pride in his upper lip. "I had to join and I wanted to join. Muslim people were all around and we had to defend ourselves."

"But you had a choice," I suggested. "You didn't have to come back."

"My family were there. Someone had to protect them. If I hadn't returned, people would have thought badly of me."

"Was there anything good about the war?"

"No. We just wanted it to stop. We didn't realise it would go on for so long. We thought it would be a short war. We didn't understand what was going on."

"Why did it continue then? Whose fault was that?"

"The outside world. We believe it went on because of them. Muslims have more rights than us now. The world believes it is all our fault, and that's not true. If the world had not got involved, the war might have stopped a long time ago."

Živorad was nodding, in eager agreement with himself. This was the official line. He could not conceive of an alternative version: another kind of past would undermine his sacrifice. His story was starting to assume a kind of form. Živorad was, I sensed, not a man of decided character. Here was a man constantly steered by the opinions of others. There was a passivity in his manner which I began to find frustrating.

"We are being pushed backwards all the time," he added petulantly.

Mrs Jovanović stood next to the bed, arms folded across her white lab coat.

"This war is not our fault," she said. "Just the people at the top."

The Director had been listening closely to her patient, attending to his answers like a teacher with a backward pupil. She explained how Živorad's son was still on the front lines, defending the honour of his family. As she talked, Živorad seemed to disappear. He withdrew from the conversation, turning his attention towards the blank window. Perhaps he thought it quite natural for other people to speak on his behalf. I turned our conversation back to Živorad and to the future.

"I will never get well," he said simply. "I will always have some disability for sure. They don't send wounded soldiers back to war."

There was relief and sadness in Živorad's voice: a national burden weighed upon him.

"You know, I would give my life for my country, for the Serb Republic. I am prepared for what I have to do. I have an obligation. I have no choice. That is the only way that war can be."

Our conversation was being noted by another patient across the ward. Momir Kosorić lay flat on his back. A spinal injury had left him in this static pose, and his angry words were directed at the roof tiles. Momir was 55, a fat man with thick flosses of white hair.

"I am ageing faster than I should because of this war," he shouted. "And you know what makes that worse? That the world sees us as aggressors!"

There were mutters of support from the nearby beds. Momir's words had provided a focus for their thoughts. I sensed a swell of dislike towards their British visitor. Before I could reply to Momir's point, the Director stepped in.

"They are right, you know," she said. "If you're with Muslims now you are not confident. They are probably thinking the same as we are. But things have changed. If you talk to a non-Serb these days, maybe a friend will come over and say you are not a good Serb."

"It's not the same as before," Momir went on. "There are Muslims here, but things are not as they used to be. We should have our country and they should have theirs. We can be neighbours, but never, never, never as before."

And then a curious thing happened. I lost my temper. Another patient in a distant bed was wailing about how Croatia had been given "the green light" to retake Krajina, and why hadn't the world helped Serbs a little more? Something flicked in my head. Several things came to the boil. The soldiers' docile views were making me irritated. An arrogant response for sure, yet I felt their anger was aimed at the wrong target. Their rage should have been directed at President Milošević for talking them into this war to start with. What's more, I was outnumbered and on the defensive.

Without much thought I shouted back. Serbia had lots of allies at the start of the war: the United States, France and Britain for a start. And don't forget Russia and Greece. Why did most of them disappear? Ask yourself that question, I retorted, before hurling accusations in my direction. Your government has to take some share of the blame. Olja the interpreter looked embarrassed. I had gone too far. Mrs Jovanović suggested we leave the ward. On the coach journey back to Belgrade, I had plenty of time to think about this splenetic outburst. Arguments erupt when two sides fail to connect, and that had certainly been the case on this occasion. My anger was like that of the Victorian trader faced with his Barrel of Stones. I had not got what I wanted, and had reacted accordingly. I thought the soldiers were intolerant, yet I had treated them in exactly the same way. There was an essential difference between our positions which neither side could bridge.

On the juddery bus, I wondered for the first time whether I would ever really understand this conflict. Parts of it would always stay out of reach, outside of my experience or comprehension. About half way though *Balkan Express*, Slavenka Drakulić came up against the same wall. The authoress was interviewing Croatian soldiers in Vukovar. After several chapters on the mental side-effects of war, the book suddenly got to the front lines, to the core of the conflict. Drakulić herself knew she was on unknown ground. "It was as if he [the soldier] was far away, and all I heard was a faint echo of his voice," she admitted. As the soldiers explained why they killed people, Drakulić realised how "the war has become the pivotal point in our lives and it determines everything else." In the end, it was not about ideas, but brute facts.

The soldiers in Banja Koviljača had spoken in nationalist clichés. But then they probably detected a few received ideas in my diatribes as well. The alternative was to take the soldiers' point of view. In order to understand that frame of mind, I would have to move into their world and accept their ideas. This was an even more contorted task. Such a stance would come dangerously close to acceptance, or even endorsement. I refused to make that kind of immoral leap. The aim was to try and keep an overview. I had to see it whole, whatever that meant.

9   Tea at The Russian Tsar

Soldiers offered one kind of answer. Another came from the victims of war. Like the other republics of the former Yugoslavia, Serbia was filled with displaced people. Accurate figures were hard to come by. Relief agencies would merely say that exiles from Croatia and Bosnia made up almost ten per cent of Serbia's population. The displaced came in expected waves: an initial flurry from Croatia in 1991-92, then the early arrivals from Bosnia. In retrospect, they were relatively fortunate. By the time around 120,000 Krajina Serbs turned up in Serbia in August 1995, local tolerance had evaporated.

That may have been one reason why I found it difficult to find people from Krajina. They seemed to vanish into the city, ashamed of their presence. The most promising source of information was a charity group called *Most*, the Serbo-Croat word for "bridge". Hundreds of families had passed through their offices looking for advice. I went there with a similar need. Amid the imported faxes and computers, there was a colourful poster laid out in greens and yellows. It was designed for children's workshops. Under the title "Rules for Fighting Fair", the poster laid out rules for good behaviour. On the left were the following list of "fouls":

> Blaming, Name Calling, Threats, Put-Downs, Bossing, Making Excuses, Not listening, Getting even, Bringing up the past, Sneering, Not taking responsibility, Hitting.

Whatever the poster's value as a teaching aid for traumatised children, the text was also a handily concise narrative on the Yugoslav conflict. There had been name calling and threats, and no end of put-downs and bossing. I had heard plenty of people bring up the past and refusing to accept responsibility. Then came the hitting.

On the right hand side of the chart there was another giggly column entitled "Calm Down"! This list had some ideas which everyone involved in the Bosnian conflict should have sat down to consider.

> Identify the problem. Focus on the problem. Attack the problem, not the person. Listen with an open mind. Treat a person's feelings with respect. Take responsibility for your actions.

At the bottom of the chart, in very small letters, was the slogan: PEACE WORKS! It was a thought.

Vanessa stood in the bookshop doorway clutching a bag of popcorn. We shook hands under a yellowing light.

"I thought you wouldn't recognise me," she said. "Belgrade is such a big place."

Her face looked pinched and wary. I guessed we were about the same age, though only in years rather than experience. She was wearing summer clothes in mid October: a navy blue and white pullover, frayed jeans and trainers. None of the garments fitted terribly well. They looked like unwanted items from someone else's wardrobe; the sardonic uniform of a refugee.

Vanessa had one question.

"Have you ever been to Knin?"

I shook my head.

"Why not?"

"Because the Serbian authorities wouldn't let us in," I said.

"That's impossible," she snapped. "We saw journalists there all the time."

"Honestly, we tried very hard."

"Well, I don't think you tried hard enough."

My credentials as a traitor clearly established, Vanessa explained how she had got to Belgrade. She was a Serb from Krajina, a refugee from Knin who had fled in the early days of

August 1995 as Croatian troops advanced on the town. That military action had brought Yugoslavia's conflict full circle. The first shots had been exchanged there in August 1990; five years on, the Croatian capture of Knin was a sign the fighting was over and the Serbian adventure had come to an end. Vanessa talked in a flat, matter-of-fact way. War seemed to have stolen some essential strength and colour from her voice. Walking through the evening streets, her toneless words were borne away by the crowd. We were both in an alien city: a place of quick strangers and foreign spaces.

"It's strange the things you bring with you," she said. "When the Croatian attack started, I ran upstairs and took out all my photo albums. I tore out all the photos, one by one. While I was up there, my father-in-law screamed 'Take some of your clothes, put them in a pillowcase...'"

Vanessa shook her head, unable to believe her actions at this distance. Surely some other person had done this.

"You do the strangest things in that situation," she went on. "I didn't take any shoes, but I grabbed all my summer dresses. I don't know what I was thinking: maybe that we were going for a few days. It was summer. We had to bring documents: ID cards, that kind of thing. And I brought one personal object: my son's umbilical cord, in a plastic dish."

"Do you like it here?" I asked.

"It may sound strange to say, but I love Zagreb much more than Belgrade," she said. "Whenever I come here, I just get the feeling that we are different."

Her husband Milan was even more lonely, she added. He was in hiding: male refugees from Krajina were still being picked up by Serb police and sent back to fight in Bosnia. As a result, Milan adopted three simple disguises to try and outwit the press gangs. First, he always went out with the children: the police would not dare to snatch him then. Second, he always wore a tie as a sign that he was from the city. Thirdly, he walked a friend's dog, another indication that he was local.

Milan's mundane disguises reflected another ugly paradox. Serbs had finally achieved their dream of living in the same country — and found they despised each other. Serbs from Serbia proper looked down on Krajina exiles: their rural manners were the butt of urbane Belgrade jokes. Those cracks had acquired a sharper edge since thousands of Krajina Serbs had started to arrive in the city. Belgraders complained of spit in the streets and foul smells on their buses. Refugees like Vanessa had become the new enemy, the symbol of national failure. Krajina Serbs did not want to stay here either.

"I know it's not smart," said Vanessa, "I know it's not safe. But I want to live and die in Knin. We used to joke long before the war that Knin was the damned valley. It's not the place with the best opportunities, but if you are born there, you will always go back."

We stopped at The Russian Tsar, an old-fashioned tea room on Republic Square. I had marched past the restaurant a week before with Vladimir Zhirinovsky. Things looked rather quieter this time. The salmon-coloured walls had been engulfed by staid portraits of Russian despots: a tribute to the link between two Orthodox countries. In Tito's time The Russian Tsar had been known simply as the Zagreb: a genteel, middle European cafe and a mark of Yugoslav tolerance. Since then, Croatia and its capital had become the enemy and awkward reminders of their shared past had to be erased. As a result, the restaurant had reverted to its original Slavic name. White-aproned waitresses still served fancy cakes and macadamized coffee, yet the Zagreb was under new management. Vanessa and I sat at a white, marble-topped table: she ordered a coffee and lit her next cigarette. By the kitchens, a bunch of bow-tied musicians were setting up for their evening cabaret. They must have remembered the Zagreb: they probably played the same melodies as before.

"In Knin, we were at the centre of things," Vanessa began. "We went to Šibenik [a town on the Dalmatian Coast] for coffee; Italy was five hours drive; Zagreb was three hours by train. It was the ideal place to live if you had money, and we had plenty of that."

Vanessa's hub sounded more like the outer rim of other people's worlds, though she was rather proud of that fact. Knin lived on in her imagination as a kind of mental handhold; its personal lustre was the only illusion she had left. There was a certainty there, a mental guard which I was not able to break. Knin had been Vanessa's playground and also her prison: the town had been her whole life. She was born there in 1966, attended its schools and then worked as a secretary to a small businessman. In 1989, she had married a local boy.

"I've looked at the wedding photographs a lot during the war. There are so many people missing from those photos."

Vanessa rested her bag of popcorn against the sugar bowl. At her invitation, I delved into the brown paper bag and extracted a pinch of pale flakes; the corn tasted cold and flavourless. It was like chewing chunks of polystyrene. When did she first know there was going to be a war, I asked.

"After the barricades went up — that must have been the Summer of 1990. Milan and I had just bought a bar outside Knin, and we were doing it up. I was pregnant then: we heard the radio reports as we were painting the building. Radio Knin told us that Croat Special Forces had gone to Benkovac [a nearby town] and taken all the weapons from the police station. We became scared because Radio Knin told us there was now a war. We didn't fear Croats in Knin, but we were afraid of the Croatian Army."

Serb-run Radio Knin had been one of the most notorious propaganda agents in the Croatian War. Over time, its listeners became possessed by dread — a change which echoed the mood swing on the Croatian side. People began to believe media tales of ethnic hatred over their own direct experiences. Radio, TV and newspaper reports were shaping a new reality which individuals found hard to resist. I wanted to know how the war started, to find its fountainhead. Vanessa recalled a chain of careless words and corrupted gestures.

"In January 1991, I went to Zagreb to visit my brother's girlfriend. I stopped in the main square to buy some little wooden dolls for her kids. The stall holder started flirting with me: he talked about how nicely I was dressed. And then he asked where

I was from. 'From Knin,' I said. That was the end of the jollity. I just paid him and there was no joking any longer. That was the last time I was in Zagreb."

"But Croats in Knin must have felt the same way," I interrupted.

"Well, yes." The words came out reluctantly.

"So what happened to them?"

"Much the same. There was one Croat woman — a friend of my mother's — who worked near our office. Sometimes she would come over for coffee and start saying 'Did you hear our President, Mr Tudjman, on television last night? When he comes here, he will do such and such....' She meant it as a joke, but of course people took her seriously and she became isolated."

I imagined a middle-aged woman, anxiously trying to fill new silences. "Why did she talk like that?" I asked.

"Why? I don't know. Perhaps if everyone around you is Serb, and you are a Croat, then you feel obliged to say something. When you feel it's forbidden, you just have to say it."

"What did she do?"

"She had to leave. She felt that pressure. They did her papers very quickly and she went to a bigger apartment in Split."

A bigger apartment. Vanessa rolled these words with venom. Everyone else had a better deal in her eyes. Did people feel guilty about forcing the woman out, I wondered.

"Not really. I mean, maybe I would do the same. Everybody was doing it."

"Why?"

"Look. Radio Knin said the Croats wanted to kill us. In that situation, you have to go and be with your people."

This was what the world had learnt to call "ethnic cleansing". Two aspects of Vanessa's account disturbed me: not just the simple act of expulsion, but the offhand way in which she described it. Yet she had been a victim too, and I guessed this was the main cause of her apparent indifference. As Vanessa had already explained, she and her family had been forced out of Knin in the summer of 1995. After three days on the summer road, they had arrived in the Bosnian Serb bastion of Banja Luka. They needed somewhere to live, so had taken part in a "house ex-change": an anodyne phrase for a coarse form of Balkan estate agency. A Croat soldier had proposed a simple swap: his house in Banja Luka for their property in Knin.

"The Croat was a real bastard," she said. "For a three-room, ground floor house seven kilometres out of Banja Luka, he got our home in Knin, my father-in-law's house and our bar."

Without warning, the cabaret band launched into "A Whiter Shade of Pale". The last time I'd heard the original was over a lounge bar pool table, killing time before a party. My memories were simple, though intact. I could return to that sea-front bar and shoot some more pool — a reassuring thread from past to present. Vanessa was shaping the ashtray contents into grey mounds and flaky trenches. We went back to 1991, the start of the war. She talked more slowly now, framing each sentence carefully as she described what happened to her husband.

"Milan wanted to leave," she said. "He tried to get out of the army. Then they arrested him, saying he was a drug dealer. When he was released, he was all blue. They beat him because he was not a good Serb. I took him to Belgrade to see a doctor: we had to keep stopping so he could be sick. His urine was full of blood. You see, they *know* how to beat people. They kick you in the back so no one can see it. They told Milan to turn towards the wall so he wouldn't see their faces. But he saw them anyway."

General Ratko Mladić had been in charge of the Yugoslav Army unit in Knin at that time. I had met General Mladić. Once. In the summer of 1993, we were in Belgrade making a documentary about the Yugoslav conflict. Our somewhat ambitious plan was to talk with the main actors in the drama while the war was still going on. Most of our requests met with flat refusals. Mladić though agreed to meet us at a battered motel in the Bosnian border town of Zvornik. The interview was full of predictable rhetoric about the "World Conspiracy Against the Serbs" and the "Islamic Population Bomb". All I could recall here in The Russian Tsar was random details: how Mladić kept a Red Cross convoy waiting outside Srebrenica for five hours while he entertained us, and how delicate his fingernails looked, as if they had just been manicured.

Vanessa sat back in her chair. The restaurant was filling up: at the next table, a young girl in flared jeans shared an ice cream with her boyfriend, passing the spoon across for alternate mouthfuls. Vanessa's attention was on a group of middle-aged men huddled near the entrance. There were five of them, all dressed in check jackets and open-necked shirts: the kind of men one always saw in cafes, mopping up their time. I figured they were businessmen, part of Belgrade's growing class of black marketeers. Some kind of meeting was taking place. Vanessa was still watching them.

"They're from Knin," she said.

"Do they know you?"

"No. But I know them. They're politicians."

She laughed and put her hand to her mouth. It was the first time I had seen her smile.

"Oh God! I'm saying all these anti-Serb things! But it doesn't matter anymore. You know, it makes me feel better when I talk. People here don't want to know. They have their own problems. So you are doing me some good too."

Vanessa's husband stayed at home, too sick for work or for the army. Knin was still relatively safe, but outlying villages were retaken by the Croats.

"1993 was not a good time to be a Croat in Knin," she said. "Serbs from the villages were coming to their doors with guns and telling them to leave. They didn't want the people you see. They wanted their homes. Most of those Serbs said nothing: they wanted a peaceful place to cope with their misery."

"Did you speak with any of them?"

"What can you say to them? There's no real argument you can use with people who are so upset and angry."

Vanessa joined the United Nations force in Knin as an interpreter. Most of her work sounded pretty dull: translating documents, sitting in while UN soldiers met their opposite numbers on the Serb side. Then there was an incident which had upset her, she said. One day in August she was sent into western Bosnia to witness an exchange of bodies between Serb and Croat soldiers.

The transaction took place in No Man's Land. Her voice softened.

"It was a very strange atmosphere. Soldiers from both sides were sitting around drinking beer. There was no fight between Serbs and Croats at that time. There were forty Serb bodies and forty Croats. None of them had been buried properly: they'd just been dumped in body bags and left there for a year. It was 30 degrees; I remember the smell."

Among the Croat soldiers, Vanessa spotted an old acquaintance from Knin. He had become the local Croat commander.

"At first, we were both nervous. Then he said how much he missed Knin. He wanted to know where people went out in the evenings; who had left, who had stayed."

I could see a summer plain. Sprinkled earth on plastic sheets. ("What did the bodies look like?" "I can't describe it").

"It was not up to him or me," she went on. "We only talked for a few minutes. At the end I said 'Give my regards to our friends in Zagreb.' And he said 'The same to my old friends in Knin.' I was glad to see him."

Vanessa smiled as she recalled her strange meeting. Her easy conversation with the Commander seemed to mock the patriotic corpses lying on the warm grass. For a moment, I glimpsed another Vanessa, an animated and talkative woman. I realised we were the same age. Then it was back to normal, as if such relaxed talk was not appropriate.

"You see, we didn't start the war. Both sides are doing bad things. But the things that are happening to your side hurt more than what's happening to the other. Once it starts, you have to take sides. You can't take a non-side. My husband tried."

Vanessa looked down at the marble table. There was one more personal detail I might like to know, she said.

"He was very good looking, that Croat guy. But we all thought he had a terrible wife. Anyway, they divorced when they got to Croatia. He told me when we were in that field."

She gave a big grin.

"We all said they would split up."

"Does it matter then?" I cut in.

"What?"

"Ultimately I mean, if you are Serb or Croat."
"It matters when it comes to war."

At seven o'clock, Vanessa got up to leave. She was meeting Milan at a friend's house and did not want to be late. We shook hands.
"I'm very fortunate," she said, without much conviction. "All my family are alive. We have a sort of house and I have a job. I am a lucky one. But then I don't feel like a refugee: I don't think about Knin, about home. I'm not strong enough to cope with it yet."
As we parted, Vanessa raised a warning finger: a country girl's advice for the big city. "Be careful here," she said. "And look after your wallet."
Vanessa stepped into the crowd. Soon she was surrounded by men in ties. Some of them walked their dogs; others hugged their children.

A few days later, the charity workers at *Most* gave me a second telephone number. There was another woman I ought to see. Natasha lived on the tenth floor of an apartment block in New Belgrade. The lifts were broken — of course — so we edged up the dark stairwell. On the eighth floor we met a young boy in a sweat shirt, smoking a cigarette. Yes, he lived here. No, he'd not heard of Natasha, though there were some refugees on the fourth floor, flat number 40. Maybe it was them, he mumbled; the numbers in this block were all wrong.
We returned to the fourth floor, with its smell of boiled vegetables and burnt something. None of the lights worked. We searched for number plates using the electronic beam of my watch; number 40 was next to an idle lift shaft.
Inside, the first thing Natasha did was show us a photograph of her old home: a big white house with a wooden balcony overlooking the Adriatic. The photograph was frayed around the edges and greased with finger marks.

"We were very well respected," she said.

Natasha was in her late thirties, a Serb teacher from Croatia's Dalmatian Coast. She was dark-skinned, Italian looking. In easier times, I could see her taking coffee at a terrace cafe, a pair of Jackie O sunglasses raised on her auburn head. She did not want me to mention her home town in case someone recognised her. "Just call it X," she said.

So what did she miss about X, I wondered.

"The sea, the climate, the city, the cleanliness" she said. "My entire life."

"Who are you now then?"

"I am a Serb from X. That's all I can say. I am a temporary Serb."

Belgrade was terrible, she went on. The children hated their school; the neighbours were rude. They lived among themselves here: grandparents and nieces crowded together in this tiny apartment for 250 marks a month. Through the kitchen door, a news bulletin ran silently on the living room tv. A map of Bosnia appeared on the screen, followed by a still photograph of Radovan Karadžić. The map of Bosnia surfaced again, then a still of President Milošević. And so on.

"I cannot find myself here," she sighed. "I felt that Croatia was in the twenty-first century and here we are back in the nineteenth. Serbia is very narrow, it's a very eastern way of living."

Our coffees had gone cold. Natasha poured the lees of each cup back into the saucepan. A batch of stale wafers were returned to their tin.

"What kind of tragic people we are. We are foreigners everywhere now."

We left Natasha some presents, the kind of sensible treats one normally gives to a sick relative: a bag of grapes and bananas, some chocolates for the kids. The children stood by the door and said Goodbye.

In the taxi, Dada asked whether I had seen the photograph album. I hadn't.

"There were pictures of Natasha at a barbecue in 1991," said Dada. "She looked really fancy. She looked really young."

10 Stars

Now and then people thought about peace, about what had been before. Duda the identical twin remembered the past whenever she picked up her address book. Some of the entries had lost their meaning. "When I look at the pages for 1987, there's no one there," she said. "All the good people have gone." Milena the academic found pathos in ordinary things. "We are a funny country," she lamented. "We build banks and petrol stations but we don't have any money or petrol." Then there was the famous film director who came face to face with Serbia's ugly new image on a visit to Italy. On arrival, the director was pulled to one side and taken to an interrogation room. "You can't come in that easily, because you're a Yugoslav," said the policeman. The director was expecting a long diatribe about the war. Instead, the policeman closed the door and embraced his captive. "Oh my friend!" he cried, "My grandfather was a fascist, my father was a fascist and I am a fascist too! How glad I am to see you!" Everyone in the city knew that story. Usually it was told as a joke; sometimes it was relayed in despair.

Others vented their sadness on the streets. Belgrade's graffiti was especially bitter, with a political sting which reminded me of Belfast. At the weekly news magazine *Vreme*, they kept a photographic file of the best retorts. Some were deftly pointed: "Mister President, why don't we have any friends?" demanded one wall. Others took a more surreal jab at Milošević: "Sloba killed Laura Palmer!"

Even the simplest messages brimmed with anger and disappointment. One student placard referred to Tito's celebrated trade: "The Locksmith was better." That jaded strain surfaced among young writers too: "I am a member of the generation which was designed for a better future," wrote author Mihajlo Pantić. "That future has now arrived in the form of an unbearable present."

Simple memories and wailing walls were a reminder that Serbs had experienced another kind of life before the war. Nationalists spoke of the historical differences which had forced South Slavs apart, yet one could also deploy history to make the opposite argument. For centuries, the Balkan peoples had lived in separate empires, with little experience of intra-regional violence. West European nations had a far worse record of local feuding — a lesson rarely heeded during the European Union's sallies into the Yugoslav conflict.

That alternative, peaceful tradition was reasserted after the Second World War. For more than forty years, Serbs lived within the bounds of the Yugoslav Federation: a political structure which allowed Serbs and Croats to live alongside other South Slav nations. Of course, the faults within that system were clear enough. Everyone knew about those. But what about its successes? Political stability gave Yugoslavs the freedom to look outwards, to expose themselves and their cultures to a wider world. When it worked, people said, the Federation worked tolerably well. Yugoslavs had one exceptional privilege over East European neighbours: they could travel freely outside their own country. As a result, Yugoslav artists and film makers became well known figures at home and abroad; the human evidence of a post-war experiment. Most of these people were still around, albeit as foreigners in their own country. I wanted to talk with them: to see why it had gone wrong, and how it might be put right.

Their stories might help explain a broader political point as well. One aspect of Serbian civic life mystified me : why such an unpopular government had not been overthrown many years ago. Serbia had lost the war and cannibalised its economy. How much more damage would Milošević need to do before he was overthrown? The answer lay as much in Serbia's confused opposition as with the President's black arts. There had been plenty of opportunities for action: street protests in 1991; legislative elections in 1992 and 1993; a Presidential campaign or two.

Yet the opposition — led by the charismatic novelist, Vuk Drašković— was in a poor state. Of course, they faced immense obstacles. State television ignored their rallies and snubbed its leaders. Politicians were attacked and insulted. At one point, Drašković was so badly beaten by state policemen that France's President Mitterrand made an official protest. But there were two critical weaknesses behind the opposition. First, Serbia's national frenzy left all politicians working to Milošević's agenda. To be against the war was to be anti-Serbian. Drašković's attacks on the war effort were somewhat undermined by his early nationalist writings and his open support for Serbs outside Serbia.

Their second flaw was one which I shared to some degree. This was a failure of vision rather than of action. On past trips to Belgrade, I had always enjoyed going out with "opposition" folk: journalists, musicians, painters and so on. We all seemed to enjoy the same films, the same music. Alongside these shared enthusiasms, I came to accept their prejudices as well. "Ordinary" Serbs were treated with undergraduate contempt. We ridiculed fans of Turbo Folk and game shows. We laughed at Milošević and his pompous aide, Borislav Jović. It was meant to sound like pride, but came out as hauteur, a refusal to engage with the everyday. By denying these objects, I had ceased to see them.

So this was a chance to explore a kind of wry fatalism — both in Serbian minds and in my own. Sitting with the soldiers in Banja Koviljaća or marching with Šešelj's nationalists, I had felt out of place and out of line. By talking to people with a similar background to my own, I was on home ground. Put in an identical position, I might have made the same decisions.

Peca Popović had the builders in when I arrived. They were fitting a pine breakfast bar into his front room and our conversation was interrupted by distant clunks and whirrs. The room housed a huge collection of vinyl records: around one thousand LPs were packed together under the hi-fi. When I voiced my admiration for this mighty gathering, Peca grinned. "Most of them are upstairs," he said. A brace of gold and platinum discs hung from the white walls.

Peca was a stocky man in his early fifties, his chin smothered by a frothy white beard. He spoke in polemical bursts, waving his hands around like a hyperactive mime artist. I warmed to him immediately. He had caught the rock and roll virus at an early age. A restive youth, Peca had stumbled into Glasgow's central station one evening in 1963 just as The Beatles arrived in the city.

"When I saw all those kids screaming and screaming," he said, "I just thought, Wow, I want to be a part of this!"

Peca played the typewriter rather better than the guitar, so he became one of Yugoslavia's first music journalists. The way he told the story now, it sounded like an enviable time: there were hazy trips abroad with Yugoslav bands like Bijelo Dugme, and a privileged life at home. Peca's large house in Dedinje was the clearest proof of that. In the mid 1980s though, Peca sensed the start of a rebellion which, for once, he did not want to be part of. Nationalism began to infect the music industry, once an arena of healthy diversity. "That was the time when things started to get un-normal," he said. After a stint as International Label Manager at state-run RTB records, Peca's career went into freefall. In 1989, he went through the next logical stage in most rock and roll careers: open heart surgery at a special hospital in Novi Sad. Since then, he had passed the time doing odd jobs and tending the garden. He grinned again.

"To be a gardener with memories, it's not bad, eh?"

The record stacks were stuffed with loving wedges of Yugoslav rock and roll. British hard rock bands were well represented too: ear-melting stuff like Led Zeppelin and Iron Maiden. There were even some punky efforts. Not surprisingly, Peca had little time for the latest home-grown product.

"Turbo Folk was sold to people as the sound of difference," he said disdainfully. "Somehow we've been manipulated into thinking that Serbs are really better than everyone else. Turbo Folk was part of the illusion that we can exist without the rest of the world.

"The striking thing about our music is that it takes different parts from different cultures. We usually borrow from our enemies — Turks, Iranians, Germans, Americans. Now, if they are our enemies, why do we use their musical strategies and their musical technology? No one ever asks that question."

It all came down to history, Peca said. I braced myself for a nationalist detour, but Peca's account was relatively level-headed. In his view, Balkan identity crises recurred because of the region's tangled history. No single empire had dominated the region long enough to successfully impose its own way of life. Everyone — the Romans, the Turks, the Habsburgs — had left traces; the result was a thoroughly mixed-up space.

"I am more and more sure that the Balkans is the biggest laboratory in mankind," said Peca. "All world ideas were first addressed on this territory. Why?"

Like all good journalists, Peca Popović answered his own questions.

"Because this is the edge of two worlds," he went on. "This is the edge of everything — between East and West — and to be close to the edge is always dangerous."

"In what way?" I interrupted.

"Well, when you are on the edge, you always try and overcome it. On the edge, nothing is original — only the edge. We've been raised with the knowledge that this part of the world is very important. You know, all ideas must come through our filter. Through them, we recognise exactly what is good and what is bad."

Now that Peca mentioned it, there was a thick streak of self-importance in national rhetoric; Momo Kapor's patriotic offerings left a pompous after-taste. One of the first clichés I had learnt about Yugoslavia was that the country perched on "an historical fault line." It seemed an uncomfortable place to sit, but some locals clearly relished living there. They enjoyed the compensation of attention. We turned back to Peca's favourite subject.

"From the 1960s to the 1980s, Yugoslavia was the bridge from the West to the East and the North. Over that bridge came Western music — rock and roll. Rock music was the last thing to be killed in this war. Musicians never believed in the national idea, and they didn't support the national parties. So the punishment was Turbo Folk."

Peca laughed sarcastically.

"So now, after all these punishments we need to go back to the world. How? Only over the best bridge. And from the very beginning that bridge was rock and roll. We must return to the bridge and try to get back into civilization: *Try*."

Peca paused and looked me in the eye, a missionary reaching the climactic point of his sermon. I felt like whispering Amen, or at least an inspiring verse of "I Love Rock and Roll". Peca probably had the original record here. We could both sing along.

"But there's a big problem," he admitted. "The new rock audience is fucked in the brain. No one here knows what's normal anymore — like is it normal to spend half my salary on electricity? No! You know, the best young part of this country is out of the country. The biggest Serbian towns outside of Yugoslavia are London and Amsterdam. How can we bring them back?"

I was about to ask the same question, but Peca got there first; he was making my job a lot easier. For a few moments, he sat still on the sofa, hands briefly at rest.

"Somebody must be very, very radical. They must say the real truth," he whispered.

"How?" I said quickly.

"The truth is that we've been involved in something that is not normal, that is not good, that is not even important! We've been told to believe that our nation is better and older than other nations. Somebody at the top must say: 'The Truth is, you are real losers. All your history, you've been real losers but you've never read your history properly. All your national myths are wrong.'

"Why can't we be normal?" he wailed. Peca's arms were back in full flight. "We must accept that our dreams are bigger than our bed. I'm afraid the quietness here at the moment is because people recognise that truth. They're starting to realise they fought under the wrong flag."

Peca shook his head.

"The biggest single problem in this damned part of the world is that every single generation must have a war. My grandfather had a war, my father had a war. I don't want to have another war."

Yet so many illusions had been abandoned: people had lost their trust in politics and the Church. How could something new be built, I asked, when faith of all kinds had disappeared. Peca added another obstacle.

"Always in the history of Serbs there has been the myth of traitors. Always. One day I realised that the number of traitors was almost equal to the number of inhabitants. So now we don't know who is a traitor, or even why they are a traitor."

The builders had left a long time ago, laying plastic shrouds over their noisy work. Peca walked over to the hi-fi and pulled out some cassettes: a few bands I might like to listen to, he said.

"When you are without jokes," he concluded, "everything is very dangerous."

As he flipped through the treasured collection, his laboured breaths filled the room.

Johnny spread his rectangle of cigarette papers on the white tablecloth and filled them with Dutch tobacco. His thin fingers moved quickly: the damp strands were teased to length and then seasoned with a gourmet portion of grass. After fashioning a roach from the hood of a Marlboro packet, Johnny lit the cigarillo and regarded it fondly. "I call this the Partisan," he said. "Because it's all for me."

I smiled, but couldn't really share his enthusiasm. Sitting on a wind-blown terrace watching a jumbo joint master class seemed a rather literal form of chilling out. Still, we were shivering in the sub-zeroes because Johnny preferred it that way, and what Johnny wanted, Johnny usually got. There were four of us crouched in the moonlight: Duda and her good friend Diego, Johnny and me. We had driven out to *Dunavski Biser* — The Pearl of the Danube — a riverside restaurant in the Zemun district of the city. As the name suggested, the Danube burbled obediently at our feet. Like most Balkan restaurants, the *Biser* was better known for entertainment rather than eats: live bands and table dancing were the only fixed dishes on the menu. Outsiders were also drawn to its low-rent charms: after a hard day at the negotiating table, diplomats and mediators liked nothing better than a hard night under it at *Dunavski Biser*. Rumour had it that when NATO jets attacked the Bosnian Serbs in the summer of 1995, Belgrade-based journalists had been somewhat slow to respond. Newsdesk inquiries met with tender silences until one reporter admitted that everyone had just wobbled home after an all-night drink-in at the *Biser*.

Inside, the party was warming up: the house band were running through a 78 rpm version of "I Shot the Sheriff". We had taken the outdoor option though because Johnny preferred to avoid people. I began to understand his reluctance when the waitress came to take our order. While the rest of us got a flash frame smile and an elsewhere gaze, Johnny was given the full treatment. The waitress, a pretty woman in her late twenties, stared at our guest as if she had seen a ghost. In a way, she had. As she scribbled down our order, her eyes kept straying to the thin, bearded man sitting on my right.

. Johnny must have looked exactly as she remembered him from ten years before: the same white shirt buttoned up to the same high collar, set off by an identical black jacket. I'd seen publicity shots from that period: even the black pigtail was the same length. Yugoslavia had moved on, but Johnny still dressed for the past: a one man resistance against the present. The waitress knew. As a teenager, she had probably posted Johnny's picture on her bedroom wall and kissed him goodnight. For in the mid-Eighties, Branimir Štulić, aka Johnny B. Štulić, had been Yugoslavia's biggest rock star, one of the last shared memories before Milošević and Tudjman nationalised their peoples' dreams.

Peca Popović had suggested I meet Johnny. "Štulić was a hero of the last days," he said fondly. "And one of our problems these days is that we are missing these big rock stars. Once upon a time we had a lot of them — and when you have enough rock stars, you have a common culture." Yet out on the terrace, Johnny refused to talk about the last days.

"Why do you want to talk about it now?" he complained. "It's too late to do anything. There's nothing more to say. Anyway, I stopped reading newspapers and watching television years ago. If things are important enough, people will tell me about them anyway."

Johnny spoke with a studied laziness. He was used to having an audience and expected our attention. Dutch exile had given his English a cozy lilt. We chattered in the sharp October air about a string of unrelated subjects: the odds of life in space (definitely), why he called his wife "mother", and Johnny's forthcoming jaunt to the Frankfurt book fair to push his Serbo-Croat translation of *The Odyssey*. He had rambling opinions on everything. Before achieving fame as a singer, Štulić had won a cult following in Zagreb as a pavement philosopher. An 800 page book, *How Johnny Spoke*, had recently come out, covering his verbal journeys from 1980 to 1995. We did not need to talk about the war, because it was there all the time, squatting at the dead centre of our conversation.

"I've done everything I ever wanted to do," Johnny said. "And what's the point of doing it anymore, since all this happened."

Johnny had sung with an innovative guitar band called Azra: their name was taken from a poem by Heinrich Heine. To me, they sounded like a Balkan version of British and American New Wave: their three minute epiphanies had an edgy, melodramatic flavour. I enjoyed the album titles even more: *When Dead Birds Fly* and *Abnormal Togetherness* sounded like sly commentaries on Yugoslav disintegration. Near the end, Johnny recorded *Balkan Rhapsody* and *The Workers Don't Believe in Happiness*. "Štulić was the first author of the days that will come," Peca had said. "Everything happened as he wrote it in his songs. And now he's the witness of the finished story."

That night on the terrace, the prophet was rather subdued. While we demolished a plate of strong Kaymak cheese, Duda told the story of Gigi, the wild drummer from Bijelo Dugme. In English, the name meant White Button — a folksy moniker to match their brand of roots rock. Gigi had helped patent the rock and roll lifestyle, but 1992 found him in Sarajevo, living with his family. For two years, he endured the city's medieval siege: I met Gigi in the autumn of 1993 and found him a distressed and desperate man: the urge to escape and the moral pressure to stay fought across his face. The following year, Duda explained, the

strain of life in Sarajevo had overwhelmed our hero. After slug-
ging several crates of beer, Gigi left home and walked towards a
disputed roadblock near Serb-run Grbavica.

There were many ways to die in Sarajevo, and this was one of
the quickest. As he approached the final checkpoint on the Bosnian side, a young soldier scrambled out of the command post
and pointed his rifle at the visitor. Gigi did not stop, and the young
lad put his finger on the trigger. Just before he started to shoot,
he let out a cry of dismay. He had recognised Gigi, and laid down
the gun.

"Gigi!" he shouted. "Don't be a fool! We need you here!"

Gigi abandoned his trip to the other side and headed back into
Sarajevo. Fame was a useful currency, even in wartime. Johnny
nodded. He had passed on the cheese.

"Gigi lives in Holland now, just like the rest of us," he said.
"If Yugoslav music has any future, it's in Amsterdam or London.
Maybe some of the bands will reform, but I can't see it happen-
ing."

Diego said that sounded like a great idea. Johnny shook his
head.

"But what's the point of speaking the same language if we
don't understand each other?" he said. "And touring was no joke
either. Whenever we played in the old days, I'd think we were
crap and the crowd would all say we were good. Then when I
thought we were good, they all thought we were crap. What can
you do? Every time I got up to sing, the fans would be there.
Before I opened my mouth, they would shout the words back at
me. And I would think, Hey hang on. Let me speak. Give me a
chance to speak."

Duda wanted to move indoors before the food froze on our
plates. Johnny still resisted, and I wondered whether there was
more to his reluctance than merely celebrity stage fright. After
all, he was a Croat — and it was not a good time for Croats to be
seen in Belgrade. When the Croatian Army moved into Krajina
in August 1995, they forced more than 120 thousand Serbs out
of their homes. Belgrade was a city with more guns than people
— and Johnny was an inviting target for someone with nothing

to lose.

Duda frowned and got up. A friend of hers was about to sing, and that clinched the argument in her mind. After some hesitation, Johnny followed. We stepped into the dining room, the air high on smoke and heat. To Johnny's dismay, Duda had claimed the only free table in the place, a four-seater at the front of the restaurant. We were a drumstick's length away from the band. Getting there meant a public walk through the overcrowded tables. Johnny waded in, head down: it was hard not to feel slightly sorry for him. As we gained the table, the band launched into a salsa version of "Can't take my eyes off you": a neat reflection of the ripple running through the distracted audience. Someone had seen Johnny and word was going around. Most of the younger people in the room were looking at the new arrival: women turned their heads, the men smiled with distant recognition. They couldn't believe it was him; this face from their forbidden, Yugoslav past. I tried to imagine what Johnny meant to them. He represented another type of past: not the virulent national saga which Serbs were being taught to believe in, but a more measured era. Johnny was the last big star. At that time, they were proud to see him as one of their own.

The man himself was gawping at the roof tiles. I followed his gaze and then realised this was Johnny's way of avoiding the eager eyes. Balkan celebrity had a long half life: the band though knew they had been completely upstaged. Duda's friend, a fat soul in a baggy Hawaiian shirt, was sweating heavily at the nape of his pigtailed neck. That was understandable: imagine knocking out "Satisfaction" on the pub Karaoke machine and then finding Mick Jagger propped up at the bar.

As the band lurched towards the chorus they lost their way, big time. The keyboard player veered off into a completely new key, playing what sounded like "Copacabana". Our man with the pigtail started to panic. "I lurve you bay-ee-bee..." came out in a flat falsetto. For a few bars, the band span off in various musical directions. Hunting for an escape route, the singer pointed his microphone at the crowd, waving it around like a hosepipe. No one from the audience joined in; the keyboard player was still ploughing up the verge. I looked at Johnny, and Johnny looked at the ceiling.

The chorus was coming round for a second mauling, when the vocalist had an inspired thought. He had seen Johnny. After no more than a crotchet rest, he pushed the mike towards his idol's face. I held my breath. Behind us, the band went on chugging away; the incident lasted a few seconds, but seemed to take much longer. Johnny took in the microphone, and then turned away. He did not do these things anymore: it was not the right time or place.

The song clattered to an end, without applause. Johnny finished his glass of cognac: he suggested it was time to leave. As the band launched into a second airing of "April in Belgrade" we made for the door, trailed by a room of disappointed faces. The event was over. Back outside, Johnny buttoned up his jacket and squinted at the black river. There was a quiet club in town he said; they played good guitar music — how about that we all went over there? Out here, the air cut against our faces; we were in the morning. Johnny gave a half smile: all of a sudden he was wide awake, ready to go.

"I don't know what to do with myself," he said.

A few days after our night out with Johnny, I had a call from Peca the journalist. He was in a rush, as usual. Two new rock bands were doing a gig at the weekend, he said. Did I want to check them out? Their names sounded intriguing enough, so they passed the first test. *Bjesovi*, which Peca roughly translated as Blackout, were sharing the bill with *Oružjem Protivu Otmićara*, Armed Against Kidnappers. Blackout were a bluesy rock combo from central Serbia, Peca explained. AAK came from the rough northern province of Vojvodina, the kind of place where their name sounded like sensible street advice. A bomb had recently exploded in a Hungarian Cultural Centre there. Hungarians were the second largest group in the province: Serb refugees from Krajina were blamed for the attack.

The only problem, Peca rattled on, was the venue. Saturday's gig was in Bor, a small town four hours drive from Belgrade. Later, I glanced at the B-roads spread across the road map like thread veins and realised that this gig came gift wrapped with a cross country rally. The prospect of a return leg early on Sunday morning added to my enthusiasm. People often said Yugoslav roads would be great — when someone got round to finishing them. Still, it was a trip out of the capital and I would be breaking new ground on the tourist front too. Bor was part of a Yugoslavia consistently ignored by travel books and coach parties. In the past, its underrated attractions had not drawn reverent crowds like Dubrovnik, Mostar or Sarajevo. Bor though had one strategic advantage over these historic towns. It was still in one piece, and free to exploit its special niche on the Balkan tourist trail as the most polluted town in the former Yugoslavia. All that Bor needed was a poet to sing its smoggy charms. Failing that, there was always me.

I agreed to meet Peca outside Metropolis Records in the centre of Belgrade. "See you there at two o'clock on Saturday," he shouted down the phone. "Opposite the UNICEF office." At this point, his voice sunk under a wave of low-tech clicks and burrs. Random words emerged from the earpiece for a while, followed by a long silence. Phone calls regularly finished this way in Serbia. There were a number of theories to account for these noises off. I thought they were part of a state-run chatline service: the best way to make new friends in Belgrade was to get a crossed line. On the other hand, the sonic drop outs could be a Serbian version of call waiting: an attempt to drive callers off the line in favour of someone higher up the *apparat* scale. Two conspiracy theories were never enough for Belgraders though. Florida Dragan said lines went dead when the secret police needed a few minutes to change their tapes — and by the way, did I know they tapped a different street every day? As for the overseas branch, well... they were more methodical. They went through countries in alphabetical order.

*

Metropolis Records was on the first floor of a flaky block, set in a weed-strewn courtyard. I had arrived early, which was my first mistake. By two-thirty there was no sign of Peca. Instead, a handful of thirty-something men had gathered in the small office, sensibly kitted out in pastel sweaters and sports jackets. Yugoslav rock critics certainly dressed the part. Three o'clock came and went without an appearance by Mr Popović; events took a brighter turn when the boss of Metropolis Records turned up. Drago Borić was short and loud; he had some good news and some bad news. The good news was that he had arrived. We all cheered. The bad news was that our bus had not. We cheered again: anything to pass the time.

I got talking with Vlada, a freelance journalist who wrote about rock music and fishing, but not necessarily at the same time. He was dressed like a teacher on his day off: grey herringbone jacket and white shirt. Most of the time, he was subtle and quizzical. Whenever the conversation turned to music however, he became passionate and engaged. During the early months of the Yugoslav war, he had escaped to London, delivering free newspapers from Knightsbridge to the Isle of Dogs.

"There's only one lesson from this war," he said. "No decent rock and roll bands have ever come out of Latin American banana republics. You see, the kids don't want, don't need rock and roll any more. They've got new heroes now: the wheeler-dealers who can turn ten German marks into ten thousand. All the money has ended up in the wrong places."

I wasn't used to hearing rock and roll cited as a force for stability: that struck at all my oldest illusions. As a vaguely rebellious teenager (school lunch hours only), I had wanted The Clash and The Damned to abolish poverty, impeach the Queen and overthrow Margaret Thatcher. Vlada saw rock music as a way of holding people together, rather than tearing them apart. We had listened to the same records and heard different messages. In a stagnant country, I had craved exotic chaos; faced with such facts in his daily life, Vlada had found a kind of serenity.

"The one thing I admire about the British music scene is its freedom," he went on. "You know, that's all thanks to your social security system. With that in place, you can play what you want and get paid for it."

Over a tin of Coke, Vlada explained how it had gone wrong in Yugoslavia. Between 1983 and 1989 more than 90 rock albums had been recorded in the Federation. Bands from Zagreb, Ljubljana and Belgrade had their own local fans, yet they also toured the country, a simple proof of the Yugoslav idea. Record sales normally had a national tilt: *Lačni Franz* (Hungry Frank) sold about half their albums in native Slovenia. The rest were bought right across Yugoslavia: rock bands were a unifying force. Specific sounds vied for attention: Two Tone's ska rhythms were popular in big industrial towns, while the guitar psalms of U2 and Simple Minds found an echo in the Croatian resort of Rijeka. It all sounded very tolerant, until Vlada pointed to one large omission. Black music — soul, reggae, dance — had never been popular in the Balkans, he said.

"Then things became tighter and tighter," he said. "Very funny things happened to mass culture. It started getting smaller and smaller."

Vlada stopped.

The gunshots came from outside: four distinct cracks from the courtyard beneath our window. Vlada looked at my taut face and laughed.

"Must be a wedding," he said.

As twenty-year-old Ford Transits go, this one was not too bad. All the wheels went round in the same direction and we even overtook a few horse-drawn carts along the way. The air conditioning came via a shrill hole in a side door. There were four of us in the back row, cramped together like kids on a school trip; the unfettered cigarette smoking added to the sense of a sixth-form awayday. Vlada had the window seat; I shared the camber with the Belgrade stringer for *Billboard*, the American music magazine. A TV producer called Nikola sat on the other side. The roads were fairly quiet: weekend couples visiting family, the occasional overloaded coach. In between towns, tractors stole along the verges. After we had been on the road for around two hours, I asked Vlada how we were doing. He pulled a face, all natural excitement gone.

"Bor is in eastern Serbia," he groaned. "It's almost in Bulgaria."

Clearly, Bulgaria came fairly low on the Serb appreciation scale. Seeing as Serbia came bottom of most other people's piles, I wondered where that left the Bulgarians. Vlada guessed we had another two hours on the road. The man from *Billboard*, a serious kind of guy, agreed. Our journey was starting to assume epic proportions: we turned back to music. Had there been any warnings of the war to come, I asked.

"Sure," said Vlada. "Serb bands were always careful when they toured on the Adriatic Coast. Some of the Croats didn't really like them. Sometimes there were fights in places like Split."

"So was Croatian music banned here during the war?"

"Not directly. I mean, there was no official ban. But then self-censorship did the same job. Everybody was insecure, and no one wanted to play anything Croatian. You just didn't."

"Why was music so important?" I interrupted.

"Because people had learned to *listen*. After five hundred years under Turkish occupation, people were used to listening to their own poems. So, lyrics were very important here. People won't listen unless they can hear something — like Johnny B Štulić."

Billboard man broke in.

"Then things started to change this summer," he said. "For four years, you didn't hear hardly any Croatian records on the radio. And then the Croats invaded Knin. Suddenly, there was this Croatian band called E.T. on the radio. It was amazing, unthinkable. That was a sign that the government wanted people to know the war was over."

Vlada was more sceptical.

"They're just trying to impose Brotherhood and Unity again," he complained. "It's got nothing to do with music."

"What about Bosnia?" I asked.

"There hasn't been any music from Bosnia for the last four years," he said.

The most polluted town in Yugoslavia came into view just before eight o'clock: we seemed to head downhill for about five miles before reaching the centre. But then I couldn't be sure: my legs had logged out an hour earlier and the rest of me was fighting off a return visit from lunch. We parked in a deserted square, spotted with broken paving stones and upturned bins. Central Bor felt rather homely in that respect: a bit like a British shopping mall on a weekday afternoon.

Falling out of the van in feverish shirtsleeves, I realised the town had one more claim to Balkan fame. It was without doubt the coldest place in Yugoslavia. A sudden fear of being stranded here with raging pneumonia made me fumble into a pullover. Never too late to go back, I told myself. Drago the Metropolis boss walked over to a pair of denim longhairs sitting on a litter bin. Grunge fashion had hit Bor about four years too late, but then there had been a war on. One of the longhairs pointed at a chunky cement pile at the back of the square.

Our venue was one of those East European amalgams of Youth Centre *cum* party headquarters. Inside, we headed straight into the most impressive cigarette haze I had seen this side of a Pathé newsreel. London in the Fifties must have looked and smelt rather like this: a nicotine pea souper in which people vanished at twenty paces. Bor had several large factories, but we had obviously stumbled on the main source of the town's pollution. Vlada, Drago and the rest were making for the lecture theatre: there was to be a quick question and answer session with local kids before the gig. I followed them into the crowded theatre.

In this part of Serbia, people knew only one Party and there was a colour poster of Slobodan Milošević above the stage as a reminder. I recognised the snap: Slobo in his Sod the World phase from 1992, all electrocuted hair and blunt menace. I took a seat in the front row, one which didn't buck around like the Ford

Transit. I figured that an hour's peace and quiet would be enough to settle my bubbly stomach before the gig. About a hundred people had turned out for the talk: mainly teenagers in flared jeans and check shirts, their fashions toned down for watchful small town streets. After the panel reached the stage, I bedded down for a quick nap.

Vlada tapped my shoulder. He was smiling.

"You're on the panel," he said.

The way Vlada explained it later on, the whole thing made perfect sense. Blackout and Armed Against Kidnappers hadn't turned up; there had been some squabble about money and they all stayed at home. So we turned into the evening's main event: six rock and roll journalists from Belgrade and this green-faced guy from Wales, England. Somehow, it seemed bad manners to admit I had never spoken at a public meeting before. And as for the Serbo-Croat, well, this would show how good the language tapes really were.

I sat next to Vlada at the far end of the stage, desperately hoping the questions would fizzle out before they reached us. The first poser came from a keen teen in the front row.

"What is the future of rock and roll in Serbia?" he demanded.

As my knowledge of Serbian pluck and twang consisted of a quick spin through Peca Popović's record collection, this was going to be tricky. I decided to take crib notes from the other speakers, and then refer to their answers. I'd seen this stunt practised at political press conferences, where it worked rather well. People were so flattered to hear their own opinions replayed to them that they forgot to listen to the answer.

A guy called Dragan Ambrozić kicked off. He edited an independent music magazine called *Ritam*, which appeared at highly irregular intervals. He was a big fan of The Fall and John Peel, so he got my vote. Dragan spoke through a shaggy curtain of hair, which meant Vlada and I could hardly hear him.

"Independent music..." he mumbled, and then I lost him, like a radio dial sliding off a station. "...Need more labels... More information about charts... Groups need to tour... Albums..."

I needed a bit more information than that. Next up was Marija Peternel, a rock journalist from Niš. Marija was rather easier to follow than Dragan: her hair was cut into a crisp, non-floppy style for a start. There were no concerts, Marija explained briskly, because everyone was short of money. I could think of two bands who proved that point. What was needed, said Marija, was cheaper tickets so kids could get into gigs. Everyone cheered and clapped. I tried to think of some similar crowd pleasing comments: maybe the offer of free one-way tickets out of Bor would get an equally ecstatic response. The man from *Billboard* made a few remarks and then the microphone appeared in front of me.

I remembered a useful rule from my days of teenage rock stardom. If in doubt, make it up. I spun some welcoming remarks in Serbo-Croat: how glad we were to be in Bor, and how great it was to see so many people here. To my ears, I sounded like a five-year-old reading out an answerphone message, though no one laughed. Well, not to my face anyway. For the more complicated sentences, I switched back shamelessly into English, leaving Vlada to interpret. Peca Popović's metaphors appeared from nowhere. Music was a bridge between East and West; we would like to hear Yugoslav music again, and then they could hear ours, etc. This may have been my first stab at public speaking, but I had seen and heard plenty of political speeches. As a result, my peroration was a crazed rhetorical canter — rock and roll will bring us all back together! Thank you! To my amazement, there was a medium-strength round of applause.

I sat back and dreamed about the journey home.

Peca and Johnny, Vlada and Dragan. There was a lot of shared ground, and a string of differences. During our painful minibus journey down to Bor, the conversation had got round to the war, as it always did. Some of the journalists took a fairly measured view of events. Others simply blamed the Croats and Bosnians and left it at that. Responsibility had to be shared by all three nations, they said. Even Peca Popović was not immune to related thoughts. He saw Serbia as a test tube for international politics: an idea which ran through the aggrieved speeches of local nationalists. That was hardly Peca's fault, though it was a reminder that ideas can have a confusing pedigree.

The line between what was good and bad had blurred: did I like Vlada or Peca any the less for their opinions? Faced with the same pressures, I doubted whether I could have made a better job of preserving my integrity. More than that, I admired their courage. To maintain any kind of alternative life in such a regimented society was admirable: Johnny Štulić's protest took the form of eloquent non-participation. Yet by his own admission, he did not know what to do with himself. Criticising the state was an empty job when no one wanted to listen. By now I had met plenty of Serbs who opposed the war. Most had made their own small accommodations with reality: a blind eye here, a complaisant mind there. Was I with Johnny, or with the crowd at *Dunavski Biser*, amazed to see this man turning up in their compromised lives? My heart said the former, but my cowardly head suspected the latter.

11 A Gap in the Head

Florida Dragan was taking me for a ride again. We were in his four-wheel-drive, scudding into Belgrade along an empty highway. Tower-blocks caught the sun, stealing the city's light. Some days, this part of town looked like a bright slice of America. Squint a little, and the azure stumps of New Belgrade turned into Californian real estate. For a moment one could escape. Then you picked up the farm carts and limping Ladas and knew we were closer to Sarajevo than to Los Angeles.

Dragan drummed the wheel with his fingers. I told him about the trip to Bor and he shook his head. Chasing old rock and roll stars was a waste of time. Things had moved on and I was rummaging in the wrong dustbins.

"You're just looking for what you like and what you know," he said sharply.

Dragan had a point. Baffled by a foreign country, I had withdrawn into a homely shell. Ligging around with rock stars and pop hacks was great fun, but they were a group apart. Too much time in their company and I would end up with a rather skewed account. It was time for a change, and Dragan had a suggestion. He wanted me to watch a video. If I really wanted to see what Serbia was like, then I had to watch his friend's documentary on organised crime. Gangsters were the new heroes, the new rock stars of Yugoslavia. These were young men who played guns rather than guitars; the kind of guys who torched restaurants after a row over the drinks tab. What swung it was the catchline. The film's title was based on every gangster's favourite farewell, *Vidimo se u Čitulji*, See You in the Obituaries.

My last brush with gang life had been in the winter of 1994. Bored with Belgrade's usual night clubs, Dada and I had toured some of the drinking boats on the banks of the River Sava. Sensible Belgraders avoided these joints: they were the rank haunts of black marketeers and mercenaries. Now and then, reports of late night shoot-outs surfaced in the local press. The bodies usually surfaced in the River Sava a little later. Blessed with a traveller's ignorance, I dismissed these accounts as scare stories and looked forward to a long night of *Rakija* and table dancing. Each bar hosted a different kind of music. One doddery boat offered Slavic ballads, while its neighbour turned out techno-dance beats. Increasingly tired and emotional, we settled in a Gypsy bar and watched a fat singer mimic sex with the help of an upright wine bottle stuffed into his waistband. With every hip grind, a fresh spurt of red wine landed on the tablecloth. This was sophisticated stuff, and it raised a laugh. Dada was less cheerful. She had spotted a local celebrity across the L-shaped cabin. I followed her gaze towards a mean-faced man in a black turtle neck. He looked like a comedy villain, the kind of character one saw in TV sitcoms or at fancy dress parties. As we watched, he folded a hundred Deutschmark note into a neat square and handed it to the juddery crooner.

"People call him Dillinger," said Dada. "For obvious reasons."

Dillinger, it turned out, was more than just a patron of the arts. He was a good friend of Arkan, aka Željko Raznatović, the man alleged to have organized acts of ethnic cleansing in Croatia and Bosnia. Tonight Dillinger seemed in a more relaxed mood, holding court with a mob of jazzy cronies. The show went on for another hour or so. Dillinger kept passing banknotes to the band, and the singer put more bottles of wine down his trousers. A young blonde in a purple mini skirt twirled on a table to gluttonous applause. Then some time around 3.00am, the mood changed. Half-way through a wild number, the Gypsy combo downed their instruments and made for the exit. On their way out, they passed a group of men having an animated discussion with the manager. Dada grabbed her shoulder bag.

"Dillinger's told those guys by the door to leave in five minutes else they'll be shot," she whispered. "I guess we should do the same."

The new arrivals sloped away before their five minutes were up. I watched the entire drama from behind a large rubber plant. That was close enough for me. After watching gang life from this front row seat, I liked the idea of reviewing it from a living room sofa. *See You in the Obituaries* had won several awards. The producers should have won a few gallantry medals too: three of the film's star turns were shot dead in the course of the filming. Director Janko Baljak had insisted that "this is a film which could only have been shot in Belgrade, in this particular time and this particular place."

Everyone was aware of the gangsters: most people knew someone who had got caught up with them. I recalled my meeting with Stanimir Ristić, the editor of a folk music magazine. Stanimir was a man of decided views. His beard was smartly trimmed and constantly distracted by a cigarette. The conversation drifted onto crime and Stanimir explained how gun lore had infected a whole generation of young men.

"My nephew, he's fourteen years old. He lives in one of those crummy apartments in New Belgrade. Dad is a caretaker, Mother stays at home. Last year, the boy started talking about this guy called Kristijan. You know, Kristijan did this, Kristijan did that. To start with, his Dad didn't pay any attention. He thought it was the usual teenage crap. Then Dad saw Kristijan in a bar — a huge, vicious man carrying a revolver. Turned out he was the biggest criminal in New Belgrade. So, Dad went home and thought a while. Everything made sense now: the flashy rings and silver crosses, the funny hours his son kept. So Dad confronted son, told him to stop hanging around with Kristijan's gang. And you know what the son said? 'Screw you Dad. Kristijan earns more in a day than you'll ever earn in a lifetime. He drives a Mercedes. You drive a Yugo'."

Stanimir had laughed for a long time. I couldn't tell whether the story made him happy or sad.

Dragan took me to his friend's house and we sat down to watch the video. *See You in the Obituaries* followed a bevy of young thugs around the city, with an occasional, despairing comment from the police chiefs trying to contain them. Gang life fed off the war and vice versa. "Because of the war, there are piles of weapons around," observed one Nenad Branković. Most of them were stolen from the front lines, then brought back to Serbia for more pressing internal battles. A policeman made the same point in reverse when he conceded they had seized enough guns and explosives from the gangsters to equip several army divisions.

Serbia's crime statistics reflected these new trends: between 1991 and 1994, the murder rate had doubled. "This is a small pond with too many crocodiles in it," observed one veteran criminal. Theft and extortion levels followed a similar upward path. "It seemed that one could do anything with impunity," said one gleeful hood, thus highlighting one of the paradoxes of war. Serbs were fighting in the name of Serbia, to defend their distinctive way of life. Yet for the duration of the conflict, the state in whose name this war was being waged had ceased to exist. The country had imploded. Peace and civil order were ditched in pursuit of the greater national good; criminals were tolerated, orderly civilians pushed to the margins.

. There was another cherishable twist to Belgrade's crime wave. One might call it the boomerang principle. Before 1991, Yugoslavia's federal authorities had an inventive way of dealing with their leading offenders. Criminals were welcome to live in Yugoslavia, as long as they plied their trade elsewhere. It was a simple enough wheeze. Itchy thugs were issued with false passports then sent off on looting trips around Europe. Sated, they returned home and spent their spoils in Balkan night clubs. Yugoslavia got all the benefits of organised crime (foreign currency, perky consumer spending) without too many of its drawbacks (executions, kidnapping, arson). Everyone was happy, save for the occasional Swedish bank or Dutch jewellery store. The former boss of police operations gave the documentary makers a fairly phlegmatic explanation. Thieves were encouraged to steal abroad, said Božidar Spasić, "so they had no need to steal here."

In 1991 though, the boomerang started its logical return leg. Barred from neighbouring countries, Yugoslav criminals had been forced to shop at home. Within a few months, the shelves were bare. They started stealing from one another, and that was when the shooting started. Janko Baljak's film chronicled this tip into madness and war fever. Some of the crimes committed had a distinctly irrational, American flavour. On the 1st December

1993, two war veterans entered an apartment in old Belgrade, looking for money. Ilija Vujić and Darko Loncarić thought the Židić family were rich. When pressed later by police, they admitted their main source of information had been an overheard conversation in a restaurant.

So the two chancers broke into the apartment, and came face to face with Verica Židić and her thirteen-year-old son, Davor. Vujić shot Mrs Židić in the liver. War had taught him that the victim lived longer that way: he thought the intense pain would make her surrender the money. Mrs Židić died before they could extract any useful information. After another argument, Vujić turned the gun on the teenage boy and shot him dead too. Police later reported there was no significant amount of money in the Židić's apartment. Like most Belgraders, their savings had been blown away in Serbia's frantic inflation. After a public hue and cry, there was a certain symmetry to the men's arrest. Someone overheard them boasting about the crime in a local restaurant. This time, the information was accurate and the two men were called in for questioning. Belgrade's police chief, Ljuba Milanović was clearly disturbed by what happened next.

"We could understand why Vujić killed the mother," he told the filmmakers. "He was trying to make her talk. But why the child? Vujić said: 'Who gives a fuck! He should have been in school.' When we heard that, I think for a couple of minutes we couldn't comprehend what he'd just told us."

The mobsters themselves did not have much to say about their chosen profession. One member of the New Belgrade gang, Mihajlo Divać volunteered that it was "fucking interesting". Another suggested the gangland tradition was part of traditional Serb culture. "Everybody knows we are a frustrated nation. We fight for reputation, for some goddamn power." Bata Trlajić, an old campaigner at 31, echoed Dragan's view that people had too little to lose. "They're all skint. Their cheapest thrill is getting a big calibre gun or a 'Scorpion' for 300 or 400 Deutschmarks, or pinching it, so they can start shooting away. It's a way out of the gloom, a way to get into the papers." This last remark was craftily overlaid with pictures of the obituary columns in the local press.

Dragan had a point. The words and deeds of these vacant warriors were a more accurate reflection of Serbia at that time than fading rock stars. They also brought me closer to the main theme: exploring and accounting for the mass violence inflicted at Srebrenica. Gangsters were one of the more extreme and visible by-products of war. They were part of what one called a "freak culture" which prized physical force over reasoned persuasion. The idol of New Belgrade, Kristijan Golubović, put that change in a blunter form. "There's no point in honest work," he declared. "People have a choice now: they either join the new élite and survive or they become isolated."

Kristijan's formula was one that all Serbs had faced during the war. Join in and get by, or stay out and push off. Everyone had made a personal decision. I understood these pressures a little better now. On past trips, I had tended to condense these equations, and assumed that everyone had made the same judgement. All Serbs were guilty for the war and that was that. At closer quarters, I could see there were degrees of responsibility, gradations of choice. Certain individuals and certain groups had more influence than others.

One of the most affecting parts of Janko Baljak's film had been his tribute to "The Wailing Wall of Departed People". A white gallery wall was covered with photographs of individuals who had fled from Serbia. According to the commentary, more than 300,000 "educated people" (their phrase) had left Serbia since 1991. While admiring their courage, I also respected the people who had stayed behind. I thought of the doctors and engineers who opposed Milošević's regime, the students and parents marching against war. There was a strain of moral courage there too.

Baljak's film was a reminder of the need to discriminate. I was in danger of blanketing an entire nation with blame. And if all were guilty to some degree, then by the same reasoning, none were especially guilty. Yet specific individuals were clearly culpable. Half-way through the documentary, a police officer got to the nub of the matter. He placed the blame for Belgrade's gang culture at the door of politicians who had encouraged state violence. "The politicians tried to build a society based on certain moral values," said the River Police Commander Milan Milenk-ović. "But those who promoted such values were not setting an example."

Milenković pointed his finger at the top. The War Crimes Tribunal had done the same by indicting the Bosnian Serb leaders Radovan Karadžić and Ratko Mladić. These were important qualifications, but how could one gauge the more diffuse sentiments found in society as a whole? One had to distinguish between different levels of guilt and responsibility. Historians had tackled such questions many times before. Did Serbia for example fit the distinctions made in Imperial Rome, where the historian Tacitus described a series of political murders that had been "dared by a few, willed by more, and tolerated by all"?

The most immediate — and also the most provocative — parallel was between Serbia and Nazi Germany. Diplomats and strategists drew comparisons between Hitler's opportunist land grabs of the late 1930s, and Milošević's plan for a "Greater Serbia". Others found unsavoury similarities between German National Socialism and Serb nationalism. Milošević's emphasis on the unique rights of Serbian people sent an atavistic shudder through Europe. Serbs responded by accusing Croatia of equally malign intentions. Hadn't President Tudjman brought back a currency unit used by Croatia's fascist government during the Second World War? They believed the Zagreb government was working with Chancellor Kohl to create a "Fourth Reich" in Europe. These fears were gaudily expressed on a poster at the Bosnian Serb press office in Belgrade. An Aryan youth stood gloating over a dead dove, a catapult in his hand. The symbolism was clumsy, as was the slogan. The peace-hating boy wore a T-shirt gilded with Croatia's red and white shield, the *šahovnica*. Behind him, a German flag billowed mightily alongside the words, *Nasty Child of a Nasty Parent*. I found the poster pathetic and offensive. But then propaganda had nothing to do with truth or objectivity: all that mattered was hammering out a brutal message.

In most people's eyes however, the symbolism was misplaced. Foreign media cast the Serbs as the Nazis of the New World Order, a form of stereotyping which they felt was reinforced by Serbian treatment of Bosnia's Muslim population. Ethnic cleansing had first come into public view during the Croatian war of 1991, when it was vigorously prosecuted by both Serbs and Croats. In Bosnia, hundreds of thousands of Muslims were forced out of their homes. Serbs felt obliged to point out that these "expulsions" affected all three sides. What they often failed to add was that Muslims were by far the largest group affected. Then came the camps: Trnopolje, Omarška, Manjaća. The discovery of several detention camps in northern Bosnia was cited as proof of an organised Serb campaign against the Republic's Muslims. People started to use the word genocide. There was no other way to describe what was happening at that time in Bosnia. Serb soldiers were carrying out a planned programme of killings. Supporters of a unified Bosnian state drew parallels with the mass murder of Jews and other minority groups by the Nazis in the Second World War. They felt there was another uncomfortable comparison in the apparent indifference of the outside world.

Europe had vowed that the scenes revealed at Auschwitz and Belsen should never be repeated. Yet once again they were being acted out on European soil.

Was it right, though, to talk about a "conventional wisdom" of anti-Muslim feeling amongst Serbs? By falling back on stock ideas of "national character" were journalists in turn misrepresenting Serb views? Reporters often described Serbs as natural fighters, as a people hardened by occupation and resistance. Such ideas have cropped up in this travelogue for one straightforward reason. Although Serbs were quick to condemn such clichés, they were often the first to use them. Without much prompting, patriots would rage against the Ottoman Empire and the Austro-Hungarian enemy. One could hardly misrepresent what was already misunderstood.

On the question of anti-Muslim feelings, I was not surprised to hear such thoughts from soldiers and nationalists: they were part of their extreme world view. More alarming was the depth of anti-Muslim sentiment in more informed circles. Jokes about Alija Izetbegović, the President of Bosnia, were swapped over dinner tables. Milošević and Tudjman got an equal pasting on these occasions, but the jibes against Izetbegović and his party followers were particularly harsh.

Bosnia's Muslims were regarded as parochial and lazy, a people without the necessary skills to compete with "superior" Serbs. When conversation turned to the Albanian Muslims of Kosovo, the slights got even cruder. Kosovo remained the most intractable Balkan knot: an Albanian majority in a province which Serbs claimed as their historic homeland. Kosovo has been amply covered by journalists and historians in recent years: a stand-off which continued to simmer but which rarely came to the boil. That said, I was solemnly told by one Belgrade liberal that Kosovans were "not to be trusted". My informer was an urbane, well-read man who had given me invaluable advice about Serbia's political scene. "Albanians are a tribal society," he said airily. "They know no other rule apart from follow-my-leader." Somehow the rest of his information now seemed tainted.

One should never pass judgement on individuals: there must always be room for a final appeal. Trying to reach a verdict about an entire nation was even more presumptuous. Could one ever deliver an assessment on something so plastic, so various? On the page, guilt and responsibility were formidable words: they carried a moral weight and shape. But when I tried to attach them to a specific time and place, they seemed to lose their definition. They were out of scale, detached from circumstance. I needed to find a more subtle instrument for measuring Serbia and its leaders. Again, there was a persuasive precedent in the ruins of Nazi Germany.

Karl Jaspers wrote *The Question of German Guilt* in 1947. In the shadow of the Nuremberg trials, he wanted to put Germany's shame within a moral context. A philosopher and writer of great clarity, Jaspers examined the question of war guilt from first principles. He started by defining the crimes which had been committed. As in a court of law, the defendant had to be accused of a specific offence before proceedings could commence. By any legal measure, Hitler's regime had seen acts of grotesque criminality. Aside from the extermination of six million Jews, the Nazis maintained a policy of terror and intimidation across large parts of occupied Europe. Jaspers also extended his definition to larger issues: the way in which the war had been fought, and even the perceived crime of starting the conflict. He wanted to isolate and identify the transgression; to understand what Primo Levi called The Nature of the Offence.

I wondered whether the crimes carried out during Yugoslavia's four-year war could be described in such a deliberate way. At the lower end of the scale, there was looting and arson — criminal acts which all three sides had committed when they got the opportunity. On a larger scale, certain incidents came to mind. There were times when the conduct of Yugoslav or Serbian troops degenerated from "defensive" to recognisably criminal. In Croatia, one only had to recall the attacks on Vukovar and the suburbs of Dubrovnik. In Bosnia, there was the persistent shelling of Sarajevo and the so-called "safe areas", and the forcible expulsion of Muslims from their homes. Surely these came within Jaspers' definition of criminal acts.

The UN's War Crimes Tribunal at The Hague had pursued the same theme. In its indictments against Radovan Karadžić and Ratko Mladić, the Tribunal had referred to specific incidents, like the siege of Sarajevo and the attack on Srebrenica. But Justice Goldstone's indictments raised a more difficult question. Was it right to concentrate on Serbian abuses when guilt was shared more widely? The bulk of Justice Goldstone's indictments were against Serbs, but charges were also laid against Croatian officers for their attacks on Muslims in Western Bosnia in 1993. These indictments related to the notorious Lašva Valley campaign. Muslim men of fighting age were sent to detention camps not unlike those run by the Bosnian Serbs.

Nationalists in Belgrade would always clutch at these parallel charges as if they somehow reduced the weight of Serbian guilt. Their attitude mirrored the defence mechanism employed by some of the accused Nazis at Nuremberg. Faced with concrete evidence of their role in war crimes, the defendants tried to diminish the offence with what historian Peter Gay called "comparative trivialization". This involved accepting that brutalities had taken place, but were relatively minor compared with the actions of other countries in the past. Thus Alfred Rosenberg told one of the Nuremberg prison psychiatrists that he could not be judged by Russians who had "30 million lives on their conscience!" Among the other defendants, there was a sense of being subjected to victor's justice. Ribbentrop tried to evade responsibility for the concentration camps with an act of moral equivalence. "Haven't you heard about how the Americans slaughtered the Indians?" he demanded. "Were they an inferior race too? — Do you know who started the concentration camps in the first place? — The British."

Serb propagandists strained towards the same argument. Soon after the detention camps were uncovered in 1992, I had lunch in London with a woman from the self-styled "Serbian Information Centre". Mrs Jovanović was a middle-aged woman with bright orange hair and a noisy tally of jewellery. Over sandwiches and tea in the British Museum's restaurant, she informed me that the "Prisoner Centres" at Trnopolje and Omarška were impeccably run places, where human rights were strictly respected. When I suggested this view ran counter to the collective evidence of eye witnesses, TV and newspaper reports and United Nations resolutions, Mrs Jovanović retreated to the standard position. These camps always existed in wartime, she said wearily: everyone had them. Within five minutes, Mrs Jovanović had moved from denying the existence of such places to actively defending them.

Jaspers' philosophical ideas were being realised in the present day by the War Crimes Tribunal. The next stage in his moral examination was to establish a coherent system of guilt. Provided there was agreement on the nature of crimes committed, could one then connect them with named individuals or groups? Some of the criminal acts seemed above the normal rules of justice. How, for example, should one judge ordinary members of the

Nazi Party, or the people who voted Hitler into power? Traditional concepts of law did not address this kind of collective shame. To this end, Jaspers proposed four types of guilt: criminal, political, moral and metaphysical. Naturally, Jaspers makes critical distinctions between each type, and stresses that some forms of transgression are more open to punishment than others. Criminal and political crimes are specific and concrete: they are triable within a court of law. The other two types have to be referred to a higher arbiter.

Jaspers' first category was relatively straightforward. "Criminal" guilt involved anyone who committed a crime within the state's laws. Such individual actions were liable to judgement within a War Crimes Court. Most of the indictments issued by The Hague Tribunal up until July 1996 came within this category. Individual foot soldiers and field commanders were charged with detailed offences. A Bosnian Serb soldier, Dušan Tadić, was accused of killing Muslims in the detention camps. Dražen Erdemović, a Bosnian Croat fighting on the Serb side, was charged with taking part in the mass killings at Srebrenica in July 1995.

Erdemović's testimony brought the War Crimes process into sharp focus. Twenty-four-year old Erdemović admitted killing between 70 to 100 Muslim men near the former UN safe area. Pleading guilty to the charges, Erdemović's defence was that he had no choice but to take part in the killings. The following account of his day in court is taken from an Associated Press wire report, May 31st 1996.

> His face flushed and apparently blinking back tears, Erdemović told presiding judge Claude Jorda of France, "Your Honour, I have told my counsel that I plead guilty."
>
> Erdemović sat slumped in his chair after entering the plea.
>
> After hearing prosecutor Eric Ostberg summarize the offences with which he is charged, Erdemović said, "Your Honour, I had to do this."
>
> "If I had refused, I would have been killed together with the victims. When I refused, they [i.e. the Serb soldiers] told me, 'If you are sorry for them, line up with them and we will kill you too.'
>
> "I am not sorry for myself, but for my family; my wife and son... then nine months. I couldn't refuse because then they would have killed me."

Erdemović then began to cry and was comforted by his attorney. But a sympathetic Jorda told him to "Get a hold of yourself and sit down."

Erdemović spoke in Serbo-Croatian.

Kill or be killed. Erdemović's defence was one faced by every Yugoslav in some form or another. At this level of inquiry, the Tribunal had some degree of success in bringing suspects to trial. But this limited legal definition of guilt satisfied the warring countries more than the Tribunal. Minor participants were coming to trial, but the most wanted figures were still at large.

Jaspers' second category was harder to pin down. "Political" guilt applied to those who had tolerated acts of violence committed by the state. This was the crime of the blind eye, of the passive observer. In Jaspers' view, all citizens are responsible for how they are governed — a right exercised most commonly through the ballot box. Everyone is therefore liable for what the state does in their name, even those who were opposed to the criminal acts involved. Translated into Serbian terms, this meant the imposition of sanctions. Of course, there were supporters and opponents. Those who had voted for Milošević or any of the extreme national parties had arguably taken a greater role in legitimising war fever than any who had supported the opposition. Figures like Milošević could only function with implicit public support. Political guilt was a consequence of this consent. I had seen it in the eyes of the teenage nationalists marching with Šešelj and Zhirinovsky. Matching sentiments had come from soldiers pinned to their hospital beds, or individuals in bars and restaurants. Even when war debts and sanctions had buckled the Serbian economy, people still saw Milošević as the best defender of their interests. Support for Milošević also implied support for his programme, and for the violent means by which it was achieved.

Jaspers' third category got to the heart of the Serbian question. "Moral" guilt involves being aware that one's actions have led to specific wrongdoing. Looking back over 12 years of Nazism, Jaspers argued that "moral failings cause the conditions out of which both crime and political guilt arise." Individuals with a clear moral sense would accept that certain actions were morally unacceptable. In Jaspers' view, Germans were guilty on this count because they had failed to prevent war crimes. I tried to apply the same principles to Serbia. People must have known about what was going on in Bosnia, yet had chosen to look the other way. This cultivated ignorance had several deeper causes. Its roots could be found in Serbia's contradictory self-image. Time and again during this journey, Serbs had drawn themselves as victims, the wronged people. Individual Serbs may have committed illegal acts, so the argument went, but that was nothing compared to the crimes inflicted on Serbs in the past and present.

Belgrade journalist Gordana Igrić had a phrase for this mass delusion. Serbs, she wrote, suffered from "a gap in the head". That cavity was enlarged by a general indifference to the war. The moral apathy one found in Serbia was encouraged by state television. Nightly news reports muffled Bosnia's war in a welter of newspeak. For two years, TV Serbia refused to mention that Sarajevo was under siege from Serb guns. The truth was only revealed when NATO jets started to attack Serb positions in the spring of 1994.

The extent of this ignorance came home to me one evening in the autumn of 1995. I had brought a VHS copy of the BBC's admirable documentary series *The Death of Yugoslavia* to Belgrade and was keen to show it to as many people as possible. For several weeks, the tape was passed from friends to friends of friends. Everyone agreed the programme was incredibly revealing. "It's a sign the war is over when people talk this openly," said one. The most intriguing reaction came from a middle-aged couple called Mira and Alex. They were Aunt and Uncle to one good friend, and were keen to see this British view of the war. Mira was an elegant woman who spoke perfect English, the result of her stint at the London Embassy in the mid 1970s. Alex was rougher, more outspoken. He wore red braces and jeans and looked like an American steelworker.

Alex took against the documentary from its first reel. As shots of Tito's funeral train rolled across the screen, he started to shout at the TV like an angry football fan. "That bloody guy," he groaned. "He was the most bloody guy." Alex kept up this commentary throughout the film, as Yugoslavia fell apart again. Rather than listen to the script, Alex preferred to add one of his own. Slovenia's astute President, Milan Kućan appeared. "Ah, this is shit," bellowed Alex. "You know he was a Serbian baby — he drank our Serbian milk! Pah — Slovenia will join the European Community and then it will be swallowed up." And so on. While Alex carried on with his florid barrage, Mira was watching closely. "So far, it's very fair," she conceded. Croatia's President Franjo Tudjman said a few words. "Ah, he's a fascist," moaned Alex. "Don't you know that the Croatian soldiers are the Army of the Pope, the Army of the Vatican?"

"Watch the programme," said Mira.

"Ah, I'm sick of this," said Alex. He stomped out of the room.

Mira looked ashamed. After a few minutes, Alex came back armed with a can of beer. By this stage, the documentary had moved away from the politicians. We were watching the early stages of the war in Bosnia: Sarajevo was being shelled and Muslims were being forcibly deported from the border town of Zvornik. Alex went silent. We watched women and children being pushed onto trucks. Their menfolk were taken elsewhere, the stark stare of fear in their eyes. Alex and Mira's living room was quiet, the cheese biscuits left uneaten on the coffee table. We had all been drawn into this cruelty. Bodies of men were piled onto a dumper truck, and Alex whispered, "I have never seen these pictures before." For the next hour and a half, he sat and watched the documentary in subdued silence. Alex had not known about these crimes. The gap in his head was too large to comprehend them. I wondered whether this revelation would change his view of the war and who was responsible for it. Alex and Mira might have taken a different view of the conflict — and their role — if they had possessed this information. On the other hand, such facts may merely have hardened their minds in favour of the conflict.

Jaspers said that jurisdiction of moral guilt lay within each person's individual conscience. Of course, that assumed individual consciences had been taught to see certain acts as immoral.

Within Serbia, that kind of re-education had not yet taken place. His final category — "metaphysical" guilt — took responsibility to a higher level. Jaspers argued that there is a general moral order which connects each human being to another. As human beings, we are generally co-responsible for acts of injustice. By standing by and allowing these events to happen, we are metaphysically culpable. Jurisdiction of metaphysical guilt lies with God.

Having drawn up these categories, Jaspers then makes an important qualification. While willing to admit that all Germans were morally and metaphysically culpable, he denies that all Germans were collectively guilty for the crimes committed by the Nazis. Collectively responsible perhaps, but not guilty. Only individuals can be punished for crimes, he points out. A whole nation cannot be charged with a crime; the criminal is always an individual. Without this critical difference, outsiders were in danger of falling into the same trap as Nazis themselves: that is, of judging whole groups by reference to some abstract "trait" or "character". "One cannot make an individual out of a people without falling victim to the same disease that affected the Nazis," wrote Klaus Fischer. "People are not evil; only individuals are."

Which brought us back to Serbia. There were individuals who had committed criminal acts. There were others who had carried out war crimes of immense brutality. Most people knew about these crimes, or at least had heard rumours about them. Few made any attempt to resist. Searching for a framework, I returned to Germany in the 1930s, and David Bankier's study of *The Germans and the Final Solution: Public Opinion under Nazism*. I did not want to make a direct comparison between The Holocaust and the fate of Bosnia's Muslim population — that would devalue two specific and harrowing events. At the same time, Bankier's conclusions on German public knowledge about the Holocaust were careful and qualified.

> There is no doubt that those who wished to know had the means at their disposal to acquire such knowledge. Those who did not or could not believe reacted so because they did not want to believe. In one sentence: they knew enough to know that it was better not to know

more... Hans Mommsen is right, then, in saying that we should ask not who knew, but who wanted to believe.

People were not born with a "gap in the head". They acquired it by forgetting rights and remembering wrongs.

12 What Zoran Saw

Zoran Petrović was a difficult man to track down and he seemed
to want it that way. I had left a telephone message for him on my
first day in Belgrade. There was no reply. In between meetings
and marches, I kept up the calls. After a while, Dada stepped in
and made some inquiries. Word came through that Zoran was too
busy filming, then he was doing some work for his research
institute. He was a busy man, or at least someone who wanted to
look like a busy man. Three weeks after my initial call, I was
lying half asleep in the hotel room when the phone rang. It was
Zoran, proposing a time and place for our interview. He sounded
tired, a little paranoid around the edges. To break the ice, I asked
how his Srebrenica material was doing. Zoran puffed and blowed
down the crinkly phone line. He mentioned a TV picture agency,
whose name I would be legally ill-advised to repeat.

"They've made thousands from my pictures," he whined. "I
will sue them one day. And when I get the money, I will give it
to humanitarian organisations, to charities."

Perhaps I paused for a little too long.

"Really, that's the truth," Zoran insisted. "I will even post date
the cheque."

This sounded like Zoran Petrović. Any man who could point
a camera at the condemned men of Srebrenica had to be somewhat hard-headed. His pictures had set me off on this trail around
Serbia, trying to make sense of the senseless. Zoran had seen it
all. He had even censored some parts of his own footage. I
recalled the sudden moments when his tape went blank, when
even Zoran had turned away. I wanted to know what he had seen
and what he had thought.

Zoran saw himself as a thinker. A journalist friend in London had
warned me of this tendency. She had interviewed Zoran soon after

the Srebrenica film was released and found him charming but vague. In the early Eighties, Zoran had won a *Le Monde* fellowship and spent a year studying in Paris, the first such student from a "Communist" country. Since then, Zoran's political thoughts had swerved violently to the right. "In 1992, he was 'eliminated' from TV Serbia because he was not a communist," wrote my London colleague. "He doesn't belong to any political party, and says he is as nationalist as the average Englishman. He identifies with De Gaulle!"

Armed with that description, I turned to the lurid material churned out by Zoran's tiny think tank. The Centre for Geopolitical Studies was run from a small office in downtown Belgrade. From there Zoran and his secretary produced pro-Serbian books and pamphlets. Some of them had reached Serb lobbyists in London. At the bottom of my office desk drawers, I kept a copy of one particularly bitter document, *Chronicle of an Announced Death*. Published in 1993, the book was a Serbian attempt to correct the media "bias" in reporting Bosnia's war. Simply put, the *Chronicle* presented Serbs as innocent victims of a concerted Croat and Muslim attack which had been planned for several years. To this end, the book reprinted gruesome pictures of Serb casualties (three heads in an ammunition box, heads without eyes, a charred body roasted on a wooden spit). There was no way of telling how accurate these pictures were, though they fitted within a well-established canon of Balkan atrocity shots. I was constantly unnerved by the graphic images used by all sides during this conflict. There was no attempt to control or sanitise casualty pictures. Supporters of press freedom would have thought this an admirable policy. At last, a war which was being reported honestly and without censorship! But for the warring parties, these bloody exhibits had a political purpose. Images of death — served up in slim coffee-table books and on television — were a way to mobilise the living, to keep the war going.

Zoran's hyperbolic essays were another way to fan that fire. In the world of Geopolitical Studies, Bosnia's Sarajevo-based government was full of Islamic fundamentalists craving to wage a *Jihad* on innocent Serbs. An essay on Bosnia's mujaheddin fighters was headlined "Iran's European Springboard". Zagreb, of course, was full of neo-Nazis. Documentation for these stirring claims was often weak or non-existent: a "confiscated" book here, a "soldier's confession" there. Under the heading, "We Cut Their Troats (sic) Until We Were Exhausted", a Bosnian soldier described joining colleagues on a killing spree. The last ten pages of Zoran's book were taken up with a literal Encyclopedia of the Dead: a "Provisional List of Victims of Moslem Terror over the Serbian People". Many of the casualties were from towns and villages around Srebrenica: scene of savage fighting in the early months of the war. One could not question the integrity of printing these names as a form of remembrance. But I wondered if the victims would have enjoyed being recalled in such an ominous way, as immortal conscripts for the next conflict.

We met one Sunday morning, in a tower block high above Belgrade. Our cinemascope view across the dormant city came courtesy of the then independent TV station, Studio B. Zoran was working in their offices. In his eyes, this was another raw deal. He always seemed to get dealt the bad cards. Or perhaps he got good hands and then played them badly. While I watched, Zoran put the finishing touches to a TV documentary on exiled writer Vladan Radoman. The programme consisted of a lengthy chat between Zoran and Mr Radoman, enlivened by patchy slabs of archive material. At one point there was a black hole of around thirty seconds, where Zoran's commentary continued without any images. "We need some pictures of that French politician Bernard Kouchner," said Zoran. "And if we can't find any stuff of him then we'll have to stick something else in." It was that kind of a programme.

We were in a drafty office on the twenty-first floor. Even to my unversed eyes, the editing gear looked antique. Every few minutes some piece of equipment would seize up or melt down, throwing Zoran into a bilingual rage. His picture editor was a gangly guy in a dirty T-shirt. Now and then the T-shirt would stop editing and wander off to some friends in the next room. This seemed to be a protest against Zoran's fractious manner. Next door they were playing *Jimi Hendrix's Greatest Hits* at top volume.

Zoran was in his late thirties, a smooth sort of man in a check jacket and turquoise polo shirt. He wore a pair of round tortoise-shell glasses. He spoke quickly and without much hesitation, his mind sandbagged by certainty. Within five minutes of our meeting, Zoran revealed (exclusively of course) that in 1992 Radovan Karadžić had asked him to become his Chief of Staff. Zoran had turned down the job because it would have damaged his "impartiality" as a journalist. "He is driven," I wrote carefully in my notebook, "and a bit mad."

In between editing traumas and Jimi Hendrix, I asked Zoran why the Serb Army had to take Srebrenica. He said it was all a trap laid by NATO in order to justify air strikes. We were back in the clotted world of conspiracies and phantoms. I repeated the question. Why did the Serbs have to take this town?

"Because even if you have a small safe area like this, you have to keep a lot of forces around it," said Zoran patiently, as if explaining basic grammar to a five-year-old. "The Serbs kept a lot of soldiers there because the Muslims kept attacking them all the time. I can give you many testimonies of this."

I let that offer pass.

"These were not safe areas," Zoran went on. "They were completely armed. The Muslims there were getting help from outside. UNPROFOR (the United Nations Protection Force) helped them all the time. They even gave them military information. Everyone denies it now, but it was obvious."

Zoran sat back in his chair, demanding my approval. This was going to be a monologue rather than a conversation.

"So you see, the Serbs had to clean that town out in order to eliminate the military menace. And they did it in a pretty humane way in my opinion."

"Hardly."

"Well, if you compare the way people were sent from that place and how Serbs were driven out of Krajina and Western Bosnia, you'll see there was an enormous difference."

Zoran had been in Srebrenica. He had filmed the buses: women and children being separated from their brothers, fathers and grandfathers. He framed soldiers firing at hillsides, rounding up prisoners. This was what he called humane.

"In 24 hours, 28,000 people left Srebrenica and went to the United Nations base. They had all the gasoline, all the cars, buses and food they needed. All there in 24 hours. And you know our people are still dying today on the roads of Bosnia! There are still bodies by the sides of the road."

Zoran had seen what he had wanted to see. He knew enough to know that it was better not to know more...*We should ask not who knew, but who wanted to believe.* Before I could step in, he deftly switched subject. There were more personal concerns to attend to. How had we obtained his pictures? More important, had we paid for them. Zoran had bills to settle, people to pay back...

"There were men passing your camera," I insisted. "And you were filming..."

"Muslim men? Yes."

"What did you think about that? You must have known they were being rounded up and were probably going to be executed"

Zoran huffed and groaned. "Of course. Look. All the journalists I've spoken with insist on this 'human feelings' thing. Yes, I saw the kids. I have two kids as well. This was a sad scene you know. You cannot be indifferent."

Zoran gave me a long stare, hoping that would strengthen his argument.

"I can assure you the Serb soldiers were touched also," he said. "Muslims may speak now of bad treatment, but I didn't see one soldier saying bad words to the poor people living in that place. Even those who carried out this operation were *more* than correct."

(Later, I recalled the scene in the field, when a middle-aged man staggered past Zoran's camera, blood plastered on his back. And I remembered the sneering words of a Serb soldier, off camera. "Oh come on, old man," said the voice. "Don't be scared. Fuck you! What are you scared of! Let's go.")

"But you were in the classic journalistic position," I said. "Couldn't you have done more to help those people?"

"Ah, 'Merciless journalist, just looking at the pictures' eh?" Zoran laughed. "I did not think too much at that moment, but I knew...when you come to such a situation, you know that it's important for history in some small way. I know that this is a document. I had to do it."

"Did you think about it afterwards?"

"Of course. But this feeling of being sorry about what happened is...well, it's not so strong after everything that happened to the Serbs."

"But at the time?"

"Well, I felt sorry for the people, because most of the people are very poor people. And in this war only the poorest are fucked completely. Most came from other regions and found refuge in Srebrenica...You see they are the peasants who don't understand what the war is about."

"Why do you say that?"

"They follow the Islamic way on a very primitive level. And they don't exactly know what is going on. I saw them as an enormous quantity, an amount of very poor people who had to change their place."

An enormous quantity. It was an unpleasant phrase, straight from the textbook of Serbian prejudices. Zoran's head was stuffed with ominous projections about alleged Muslim promiscuity and Croat savagery. Such nostrums supported his mental universe and filled his own publications. To me, such ideas sounded bigoted and grossly offensive. Zoran took a showy pride in his intelligence — he talked of "humanistic discourse" and the "geopolitical situation" — but he had not trained it on his own illusions.

"I remember one very strong feeling," he went on, "even with this feeling of general sorrow. I saw many kids there from zero to three years old."

"What does that mean?"

"That means a lot. It means that even in those conditions of extreme poverty and lack of food and certainty, among 28,000 people there were almost 8,000 kids aged zero to three years old."

"Who told you that?"

"Officials. On the Serbian side."

"And you believed them?"

"Yes. I mean the Muslims were doing their demographic task. It's completely crazy to make 8,000 kids in three years of being surrounded in this area without food."

Others might think the figures themselves were somewhat crazy. There was no way of verifying them. They sounded like the product of propaganda rather than secure facts. Serb soldiers needed these arguments in order to attack the town. Zoran pushed on, enlarging his hysterical theme.

"This was the work of the religious authorities you know. My reaction to being surrounded would not be to make two, three or four kids. It's very difficult to explain to people from Western countries."

He was right on that point. This would all prove very difficult to explain when Zoran was called as a witness by the UN's War Crimes Tribunal.

"You make Muslims sound like monsters, not like normal people" I said.

Zoran shook his head.

"No. I just account for this by their social organisation. In primitive parts of western Bosnia, they simply follow the priest. This is the absolute truth. They don't think about it. 8,000 babies. Just think about it."

"You keep mentioning that figure. Why are you so sure about it?"

"Because I was with the officials who had all the figures of the situation in the refugee camps. And I check things like that you know."

"How?"

"Well, I believed it because the kids I saw were very numerous. There were lots of old people and lots of young people you know."

"But wasn't that because all the men had been taken away? There were only women and children left."

Zoran hesitated.

"We have to make a separation between language at a geopolitical level and what we feel privately, at a human level," he said mysteriously. It was not quite the answer I was hoping for. Perhaps these were not the questions Zoran had hoped for either. Sensing that his patriotic homilies were not working, Zoran tried a different approach.

"Look, if you're normal you can't be indifferent towards this. Because you see people who are in a weak position. It would be the same if you were in Sarajevo and somebody was throwing grenades at you. You are with the people who are in Sarajevo. Because you don't see when Muslims from Sarajevo are firing on the Serbs. You're not interested in this. You see just one fragment of the solution. Now if I see one fragment in Srebrenica, then I must feel big sorrow for the people. It's normal you know. The Special Forces said so too."

The Special Forces. Zoran dropped that phrase in because he wanted it to be picked up. I tried to look impressed. Zoran was clearly proud of this connection. These contacts had got him into Srebrenica. Once there, he had gained an "exclusive": the only journalist to film the early stages of a massacre. He wanted to advertise that fact.

"How did you get in then?" I asked. Zoran turned modest.

"Oh, I found the people and went in with them. They were Special Forces from the *Republika Srpska*. All very well educated men."

Most Serbs in Belgrade now looked down on Radovan Karadžić's tinpot state as an embarassment. Zoran would have none of it. Dr Karadžić's would-be chief of staff was a huge admirer of the *Republika Srpska* and its militant leader.

"I am with them privately because they are trying to build a future society which will be very similar to England or America," he said.

"In what ways?" I choked.

"In political institutions first of all. It's a non-Communist country, with a parliamentary democracy and a rule of law. All of which is not in Belgrade."

And not in the *Republika Srpska* either, I thought.

"I still think their cause is just," Zoran went on. "It's a fight for self-determination which is always denied to Serbs in the Balkans."

Keen for conspiracy, Zoran hinted there was a "longer story" to tell about how Milošević had betrayed the Bosnian Serbs. Peering over his glasses, he offered to show me "documents" which proved this claim. Zoran's fierce assertions were a reminder that Serb nationalism had its own peculiar divisions and loyalties. Some of the leading Serbs in Bosnia looked down on their "Communist" patrons in Belgrade, and yearned for a return to Monarchy and sharp capitalist practises. For Zoran, this presented a double obstacle. Outsiders like myself refused to believe his yarns. A lot of Serbs on the Serbian side of the border felt the same way.

"There are a lot of people in Belgrade who think I produced propaganda in Srebrenica," he said. "But when I ask them what was propaganda in that story, they have no answer, you know. I was very careful to work within the strict deontology of the profession. Sure, I worked on the Serbian side. Only a few journalists can cover both sides. You know, that funny man in a white coat on the BBC — what's his name?"

"Martin Bell."

"Mr Bell. Yes, well he can report from all sides. Like Sky or CNN. Now I was very careful not to say one lie. If anyone can prove one lie in my work, I will say 'Bravo'..."

This seemed as good a time as any to mention the lens cap. Zoran had stopped editing the Studio B documentary altogether by this point. His editor had left the room, leaving the two of us with a set of humming video machines. I thought back to my first viewing of Zoran's film a few months earlier. Serb soldiers lying by the road, pistols ready. A marksman wreathed in bandoleers, and then Zoran's whip pan around to a group of Muslim men gathered in a clearing. They had been rounded up. Instinct suggested the Serb soldiers were about to do something. And then Zoran had wiped the tape. A black hole without any commentary.

"That part of the tape when you filmed the prisoners at the roadside..."

"The Muslims, yeah."

"Why did you erase those pictures? There's just audio on the tape, no pictures. Why did you wipe that part?"

Zoran's voice thickened. He had rehearsed this defence several times before. It had a planned precision.

"Look, I had just ten seconds which were blank. I decided to do that for two reasons. One, it was for the guys who brought me there. If I had used those pictures, it would have put them in an even harder situation. I was in an illegal situation..."

"Illegal?"

"Because there was a strict order not to film prisoners, and I had already done that. So when the camera moved out to see the whole of the group, I did it without.."

Permission was the word Zoran was looking for. Then he switched focus, moving to a wider view.

"Professionally, it was hard for me because it was a very interesting scene. There were more Muslims there. But I arrived three hours after General Mladić and I knew that his camera crew had filmed everything."

Earlier, Zoran had stressed how important it was to be a witness. Yet at the critical moment, he had stopped filming.

"Why did you put the camera down?" I asked.

"Well, I wanted to show my hosts — knowing this situation — that I respected the rules and I just filmed a little. Because you know that journalists always want to do more than is permitted. I satisfied myself. And for the people on the spot, it was very important that I didn't break the rules."

"And what were the rules?"

"Listen, I had more freedom there than your English journalists had in the Falklands War. Because I was on the spot. They didn't need to put me there, militarily speaking."

"So what happened to those prisoners?"

"I can guarantee to you, I can say it ten times. Nobody was killed there among those people on the road. Just technically, I wanted to respect my hosts."

"And what went on during that ten to fifteen second gap?"

"In that fifteen seconds, my camera goes from the guy who is screaming to the people who were sitting there. I didn't want to make problems for myself. I couldn't promenade there, you understand. There were military rules."

Zoran had returned my questions with a fresh set of queries. His own feelings were disguised behind a double veil of nationalism and professional duty. Journalism demanded a certain distance, and there was no obligation to feel pity. But surely this was one occasion on which basic human emotions would have played a part. Perhaps Zoran thought that got in the way of "the story." The telephone gave out a feeble ring. I stopped my tape recorder.

When we came back, Zoran stonewalled a few more questions about Srebrenica. Like a veteran politician, his answers suggested a great deal while offering little. Along the way, Zoran the thinker was keen to inflict some of his political theories. He talked of America's "New Internationalism" and the NATO force being sent to Bosnia. US generals in the Pentagon had wanted to weaken Yugoslavia, "to put the Serbs in order". Croatian army generals had been kidnapped by the CIA and brainwashed in Frankfurt. And so on. As proof, Zoran showed me an article in a very obscure American foreign policy journal. The relevant piece was covered in angry dashes of red pen, like a teacher's marks in an exercise book. These were Zoran's own animated annotations. Each margin was clogged up with red exclamation marks: two here, three there. As he meandered on, I felt my brain starting to seal over. (In an attempt to stay awake, I wrote some notes: "This sounds like rubbish to me, and he thinks I'm talking rubbish, so it's quite a conversation.")

"I can guarantee you I know much more than most of the political leaders," Zoran said. "You will never have anybody doing a geopolitical analysis of the situation. Never."

"But the basic problem is simple enough," I volunteered, desperate for air. "Serbs are divided amongst themselves. Then they try and blame others for the division."

"Sure. But that's partly our mentality. Everybody wants to be a Chief. Everybody thinks they are the most intelligent. Everybody wants power. What's more, it's not a sin here to do over your brother, if it's really necessary."

Our talk was starting to go round in circles. Zoran showed no inclination to return to his work, so I guessed we were stuck here for a while. Why, I wondered, did we see events in such different lights? Where he saw a conspiracy, I usually found a cock up. Zoran gave me a condescending look.

"I think the Western way of analysing events is rather, ah, superficial," he said. "You don't introduce important elements into your scenario. From the start, it was a war of terminology. Sure, some crimes did happen. This is a war. Terrible things occurred, but not on the level the Western media presents it. Not even close to this."

Suitably rebuffed, I sat back and listened some more. Zoran kept repeating his points in slightly different forms. When he hinted that he wanted to get on with his documentary, I made swift moves for the door. Just to make sure I had understood his points, Zoran walked me to the lift and rode down to reception. The cameraman assumed a yellow tinge in the poor light of the elevator. He took my Belgrade address and promised to send over his Institute's latest pamphlets.

"You know, a Professor of International Relations came to our centre last month," he said. "From Boston University."

I made an impressed hum. Our lift jumped to a halt on the ground floor.

"And you know, I was astonished. He looked at our research and then said to me, 'Oh, don't be so convinced. The Americans don't know what they're doing really.' He was very naive."

It was time to go.

13   Tito's Secretary

October turned into November. Above our heads, the plot was changing. An American team had been shuttling around the Balkans and had pieced together some kind of deal. Someone talked about a truce. Richard Holbrooke, the sharp-elbowed Assistant Secretary of State announced that all sides would be going to Dayton, Ohio to hammer out a peace agreement. They had a date and an agenda. Holbrooke's strategy was insultingly simple: intern all three leaders in an empty US airbase until they find a solution. He called them "proximity talks". The Belgrade press complained that their leaders were being treated like awkward kids. Others felt that all things considered, this was rather a generous way to handle them. Even so, hopes were hardly high.

People had lost count of the number of failed ceasefires in Bosnia. It was like the old gag about the man who had no problems giving up smoking. After all he'd done it hundreds of times. Bosnian scepticism was borne of experience: at Sarajevo airport, I had seen a sniper screen defaced with a wobbly piece of graffiti: "18.03.93: 1200 hrs — ceasefire lasted 13.65 seconds."

This time though, there was a difference. The Americans were in charge rather than the Europeans, and that satisfied the Balkan Presidents. It gave their squabble a bloody seal of approval: they had sired a conflict so intractable that only a superpower could solve it. Yugoslavia was now up there with those other gridlocks like the Middle East and Northern Ireland. Everyone's honour could be satisfied. Perhaps pride had been behind this conflict all along. Yugoslavs from each nation talked fondly of the time when their country was a notable force. They remembered the non-aligned movement and Tito's leathery charisma. In essence, the war had been a search for such attention on a national scale. When the three leaders trouped into Dayton airbase a few weeks later, they finally achieved that goal.

A kind of peace was in the air. No one was quite sure what this meant. Would Serbia continue with its national project, even after a string of defeats in Bosnia and Croatia? That did not seem a viable option for President Milošević: it would invite familiar accusations of betrayal. Back to the Future had always been Milošević's favourite tactic, and as Dayton took shape, a new policy began to emerge. Having plundered Serbia's national past for ideas, Milošević and his supporters at TV Serbia performed a surreal turnaround. Tito was back in fashion. Yugoslavia and its fraternal ideals had been destroyed in order to wage war: now they had to be reinvented to help cement a peace. The most blatant vehicle for this exercise was an organisation called JUL: the Yugoslav Union of the Left. JUL presented itself as a supposedly social democratic party: a tolerant "European" movement which had no time for nationalism. It was a fresh start, a return to Tito's Yugoslav dreams. Playwrights and academics signed up, even though they had their doubts. Well, one doubt in particular. In the land of planned spontaneity, even JUL served a larger aim. The movement's President was one Mira Marković, wife of Serbia's inventive leader, Slobodan Milošević.

As for Tito himself, he hadn't fared too well since his funeral. When the wily locksmith died in 1980, a new slogan was coined for his grieving people: *After Tito, Tito.* There was a shade of desperation in these words. They sounded like a nursery chant: comforting in their repetition but undeniably empty. As Yugoslavia's most prominent republics drifted towards national solutions, the mantra was abandoned along with its venerable relative, *Brotherhood and Unity.* Yugoslavia's bolt into the past showed that people either had very short memories or impossibly long ones, depending on your perspective. Fifteen years on there were hardly any traces left in Belgrade of Tito's personality cult: the new regime had covered his foundations. On a previous trip, I had visited Tito's Mausoleum high above the city, and was keen to make a return call. According to my Belgrade guide book, Tito's tomb was behind the 25th May Museum on *Bulevar Mira,* the Boulevard of Peace. His museum was a shrine to the "Marshal Liberator", a splendid example of party verbiage. Each year on the 25th May, a relay of Yugoslav children had run through the Federation with a white baton, symbolising their country's unity. My old guide book claimed the batons were on display in *Bulevar Mira* along with gifts donated to the Yugoslav leader. Tito's courtiers said he received an average of eight presents each day. A more cynical observer said they were "displayed in the Oriental fashion of Emperors at the centre of the world."

My problems started at the hotel reception desk. Neither of the chaps on duty knew how to find *Bulevar Mira*. One of them, a bulbous man in his fifties, frowned at the tourist map.

"I know that name," he said helpfully. "The road's here somewhere." He moved his face close to the page, as if one could sniff out the relevant street.

"It's near Dedinje," I volunteered.

"Yes, I know. It's somewhere on here. God! I used to know."

Keen to help, I mentioned the Tito Museum, you know, 25th May... Enlightenment shot across Mr Bulbous's face.

"Ah! *Bulevar Octobarske Revolucije*. Yes, yes — they changed the name a couple of years ago, along with all the other big streets."

"Why?"

"Well... because of the things going on in Bosnia"

"That's very confusing."

"Sure it is. But..." Mr Bulbous trailed off.

Everything was clear. I was looking for the relics of a man who no longer existed, in a street which had lost its name. Everyone talked about the past, but only when it fitted into the present.

These days, people told jokes against Tito. On the van ride down to Bor, Vlada the rock journalist had talked about Tito's increasingly odd behaviour in his final years. One evening late in the 1970s, Tito had visited the town of Kraljevo to address a huge meeting. As the crowd cheered, Tito walked up to the podium and adjusted the microphone. The cheers died down and the leader

cleared his throat.
  "Good evening — Kragujevac!" he shouted.
  "And do you know what?" said Vlada. "Everyone laughed.
Tito was senile, he got names wrong all the time. But no one
wanted to admit that, so they all pretended he'd made a brilliant
joke."

The path was made of neat square stones, so smooth they looked
almost new. I walked slowly, pretending to reverence. On the
right was a concrete amphitheatre. A thousand school trips had
been here: their presence marked by childish scrawls on stone.
For a Monday morning, the 25th May Museum was doing a poor
trade. There were two of us in the cloudy sun, and only one of us
looked like a punter. Up ahead, a white whiskered man sat on a
wooden bench examining the paving slabs.
  His Sunday suit and parlour shoes seemed out of place here.
I guessed he was a visitor too; another country man washed up
on the city strand. Above us, crows chatted in the heaving trees.
At the top of the path lay a squat building which reminded me of
an airport arrivals hall: a dated confection of rectangular glass
and jutting cement. The front was dominated by a naive mural,
rendered in earthy brown and grey. A trio of stick soldiers stood
next to three women, pushing what looked like barrels of food.
Yugoslavia's old red star was the only pulse of colour. There was
an artificial air about the place. I felt like a guest in an oversized
front room, the kind of unloved, unlived space where one came
for special occasions.
  The entrance was locked. A typewritten note of the opening
hours had been pasted to a side window. Scanning the page, I saw
a pale figure through the dulled glass. He was watching me,
hoping I had not seen his idle shadow. After a brief dumb show,
the man shuffled reluctantly to the door: a caretaker in shiny blue
suit and slack tie.
  "Don't you understand?" he said, speaking Serbian slowly for
my benefit. "The gallery's not open today."
  "Is this the 25th May Museum?"

"Yes," he said. "But it's not here."

"What?"

"The 25th May Museum is not here."

"Where is it?"

A shrug. The caretaker looked confused.

"It went. "

"When?"

"Before the war. '89 or so. Maybe 1990. I don't know."

"Who removed it?"

"The authorities here in Belgrade. I don't know where it's all gone — somewhere in the city."

"Why?"

"Look, it's not here. If you want the gallery, come back tomorrow."

At the Mausoleum entrance, it was the same story. Tito's grave was closed for the day and no, I could not have a special visit. Down below, the elderly man in black stood up and spat hard at the ground. A young woman with shopping bags passed the amphitheatre; Tito's resting place was a handy short cut. I turned back to *Bulevar Mira*. Beneath my feet was a concrete path, divided into two lanes like a motorway. One lane had a white arrow pointing up to the Mausoleum, the other arrow led down to the road. Both aisles had been designed for mass visits, as a way to coordinate thousands of mourners. That was the past. Heading for the car park, I jumped from one side of the lines to another: going up and going down. There was no need to obey these instructions anymore.

I stood on the stairwell and waited. Three locks shot back and a white door was pulled open. For a moment, I caught myself smiling into space. "Ah, a big English boy," said a voice from somewhere around the door handle. Jara Ribnikar was a lot shorter than I had expected. Looking down, I saw a fair-haired woman with vivid, darting eyes and a wide smile. She was eighty years old, but looked ten years younger. Mrs Ribnikar lived on General Ždanova street in the centre of Belgrade. Her apartment curved round a deep courtyard, lined with Friday washing.

"We'll go in the drawing room," she said, and led me into a gloomy chamber. We sat on opposite sides of a wooden table, the noise of Belgrade's inner city at a subtle distance. I had come here to talk about the war, but Jara had some questions of her own. Who had I met in Belgrade, and what did I make of them? Had I met Zvonimir X and Mirjana Y? She would arrange introductions; I could not leave Serbia without seeing them. These were the kind of florid queries one normally got at a party or a reception. After all, that was Jara Ribnikar's world.

The lady facing me in a navy blue blouse and tartan skirt was part of Belgrade's past as well as its present. Jara Ribnikar had worked alongside Tito during the Second World War. She knew all of the President's friends and enemies too: the veteran dissident Milovan Djilas had been a close companion. For fifty years, Jara and her late husband Vladislav had been at the smart hub of Belgrade's political and cultural life. Vladislav had edited *Politika* which had been a better paper before people started fiddling with weather maps and horoscopes. Jara translated novels and was a well known author in her own right. Even today's politicians knew her value: she was on the advisory committee of Mira Marković's political vehicle, JUL. While I munched through a plate of pears stewed in a treacly sauce, Jara offered her thoughts on war and the chances of peace at Dayton.

"Yugoslavia worked you know." Her voice was soft but clear, a voice that was used to winning attention. "Yugoslavia worked very well, but it broke down over the economy. Now what do we have? The Slovenians find food is expensive when they have to buy it from Italy. They have enough fish and wine, but you can't live on that. They need Serbia for their basic foodstuffs. That's why Yugoslavia was the ideal economic collaboration."

The chairs were hard. I moved around, trying to gain some comfort. Jara frowned as she thought of national stupidity.

"People here always say 'It will never be as it was before.' But it will be. It *has* to be."

"But after this war? Surely it will be difficult."

"Don't be so sure. Soon there will be easier frontiers, and then there will be trade delegations. A little later — a year or so, there will be a new Yugoslav passport for Serbs, Slovenes and Croats. It'll start with businessmen, then sportsmen and artists."

"Doesn't that take everyone back to where they started?"

"No. It won't be a Federation. The countries want their embassies — they all like going to conferences. So why create one state where there could be five? They will all work together for what they need, but they will also have their independence. It's so easy because we all have the same language."

Four years of war so that each republic could have an embassy and a seat at the conference table. A worldly judgement. Certainly one which could only be made by someone well away from the conflict, I thought. Then Mrs Ribnikar paused, as if her first thoughts were not her true thoughts. She looked into the coffee, and offered a different answer.

."Life is crazy here now, you know. There are no more normal people around."

"What's normal now?" I interrupted.

"Normal is to be not neurotic," she said carefully. "Now every second person here is neurotic. People are melancholic."

"And the future?"

"I'm afraid the war will never finish. At Dayton, they will officially end the Bosnian war. But there are still all these unofficial groups who will make provocations: people who have lost members of their family, who feel they must have revenge."

This sounded like a more realistic view, a better reflection of Mrs Ribnikar's experience. Pouring two viscous coffees into white china cups, she explained how her family had come to Belgrade in 1933. "There were only two kilometres of asphalt road here when we arrived. The rest was cobbled." Jara's family came from Eastern Bohemia, in what became Czechoslovakia. Her father was a pianist. As Professor of Music at the Belgrade Academy, he gave young Jara an instant entry into the city's cultural life.

"I came into the élite of the intellectuals. I must thank all those people for helping me to create myself. You cannot create yourself alone."

The nationalist writer Momo Kapor had spoken fondly of Jara Ribnikar. She was charismatic and energetic, he said. I found her charming too, though I sensed that charm was being used for a specific purpose. Like many of my other friends, Jara wanted to correct my impressions of Serbia. There was an evangelizing streak which I felt obliged to resist. Her first impressions of Belgrade had been formed in a time of relative peace. Mine had been created during a war.

"I was very impressed with Belgrade," she said. "Serbians are very talented people."

Mrs Ribnikar anticipated the next question, her eyes following my writing hand across the notebook.

"I can't speak about Croats or Bosnians," she said, "because I haven't lived there. People here are stronger because they're always fighting for their life. They tried to be cleverer than the Turks, and fought them for centuries. The old kings always thought of ways to survive. There was a historical gymnasty of brains here. The Serbian intelligence is like an instrument, like a vibration. It's very sensitive. Sometimes they're so clever that I don't like it."

The drawing room was losing light. We were sitting in a cold mist of greys and browns. I could understand the reasons for Jara Ribnikar's love of Serbia, without wanting to share all of them. We were back to that friendly analogy about current affairs and theatre. We had entered the Balkan theatre during different acts, and that naturally affected our perspective. I confessed to being allergic to nationalism. Jara shrugged her small shoulders.

"It's bad, of course. But I can understand these emotions. I can't comprehend them, but I understand them. There have been so many lies about Serbs. In war time, pathological instincts come to the surface, you know."

"Tell me about Tito," I said.

Jara's face relaxed and let in light.

"People said he came from Mars. They worshipped him: he was not like other people. He was an ordinary man and an extraordinary man at the same moment."

Jara was back in the Bosnian town of Drvar in April 1944.

She had volunteered to work as one of Tito's secretaries in his days as Partisan leader. They had lived in the mountains, hiding from German patrols in a humid cave. After the war, Jara and her husband had joined Tito at his various retreats: a small hunting lodge in Vojvodina was their favourite. "It was a hard time, but a wonderful time. We were happy. Working, working."

She was looking out of the drawing room window, into the afternoon courtyard. As if Tito were there, as if he were watching and listening. By now the light was so thin that my notes looked like pages of ink washed in water. Jara found an electric fire at her feet and switched on one orange bar.

"This isn't new, this isolation," she said. "We've been treated like this before. Soon after Tito broke from Stalin in 1948, I was in Paris for a conference. I hailed a taxi and asked to be taken to the Yugoslav Embassy, Boulevard de la Serre. Suddenly, the driver stopped the car and asked me to get out. He was a member of the French Communist Party, someone who supported the Soviet Union. 'Get out!' he shouted. 'I don't take Yugoslav communists in my cab.' So I pulled all my bags out, and sat on my own by the roadside."

Jara smiled.

"So there you are," she said.

14 Outside the Barrel

At this stage of the game, most readers expect certain things to happen. The journey is about to end: loose scraps of fact and fiction have to be tidied up, themes spun into a pleasing pattern. There has to be an ending, a sense of completion. My first stab at this final chapter went along these lines. It didn't work somehow. The sentences were too frenetic, too eager for meaning. At first, I thought this was a journalist's flaw: the urge to push everything into the mix, to report everything and nothing. Then I wondered whether Serbia had left its own imprint. The rash remarks and choppy platitudes: I was starting to think like a nationalist myself. Yet if there was one thing I had learnt it was that nations could not be poured into a standard mould or reduced to alarming facts.

Perhaps I had been in Belgrade for too long. I left the day after the assassination of Israel's Prime Minister Yitzhak Rabin. I packed my suitcase to the soundtrack of trouble: televised sirens and replayed gunshots. Yugoslavia seemed a tolerable place by comparison. For a moment it was calmer than the Middle East, where peace makers were gunned down at public meetings.

The first draft went on in a similar vein. I whined about the 50 Deutschmark "airport tax" slapped on my ticket at Belgrade check in. I howled when our plane was slightly delayed. I even wrung some false drama from the confiscation of my passport — taken away for examination behind double-sided mirrors. And then I figured this was a waste of space. No one really wanted to know. Everyone has read that kind of stuff before: most have been through it themselves. That's another payoff from mass tourism: there are not enough traveller's tales left. They've all been worn down, a devalued currency.

No. There were more interesting things to report. Like how strange Heathrow felt after a month in the Balkans. Britain was the foreign country now, not Serbia. Walking through the franchised frenzy of Terminal Two, the native phrases and gestures felt false and alien. There was a coded politeness in the tie stores and perfume marts, a quality which had been mostly absent on Belgrade's rowdy streets. It felt laughably fussy after Serbia's rough vitality.

After a month of struggling in a second tongue, I was back in my own language, a swimmer returning gratefully to his small pond. What struck me straight away was the relative richness and complexity of visual life. Adverts in particular had a dense allusiveness missing in Serbia. Most ads in Belgrade — either on TV or on roadside hoardings — were dismally simple. Meat suppliers were promoted with drab snaps of dead meat, shot with all the flair of a mail order catalogue. Starved of visual invention, I thought the billboards around Heathrow were oddly exciting, as were their brittle promises. Credit cards! Luxury cars! Diet Coke! I looked at them with the same vague excitement as a child. Normally I would dismiss these plastic demands, but absence had made me innocent.

I had returned from a disturbed country, where people were routinely judged by their supposed "ethnic" group rather than their character. Coming home, I was aware that my natural disgust for these attitudes was undermined by a furtive prejudice of my own. At the back of my mind was a belief that British tolerance was markedly superior to the strain found in the former Yugoslavia. In other words, I had started to see Serbs as racist bigots, and British folk as nice, tolerant people. Of course, there were plenty of people within the UK who would dispute that view. After my first encounter at Heathrow that afternoon, I was ready to rejoin them.

Needing a rail ticket to get home, I went to the British Rail desk at the back of Terminal Two arrivals. A small queue had formed behind a stooping, middle aged man in a heavy green overcoat. The visitor sounded German or Austrian, and appeared to be in some trouble: what was the quickest way to get to Euston station? What time did the last train for Birmingham leave London? These sounded like sensible questions, the kind of requests which filled every hour at a ticket counter. But what appalled me was the laboured rudeness of the clerk behind the desk. He was about the same age as his German customer, but white and turkey-skinned from too little sun. Every question was greeted with a melodramatic sigh or a clipped reply. "Well, that's your problem isn't it," said the clerk at one point. After a five minute stand-off the tourist walked off, having been handed a tiny timetable. The unspoken message was: work it out for yourself. As the queue had thinned out somewhat, I was next in line. The clerk scowled at me, expecting another difficult customer. As soon as he heard my homely accent, his face changed.

"Let's have a look through the timetables then," he said promptly. "Shouldn't be a problem."

Dealing with one of his own, the clerk had become a different person. He showed me a better face. I was ashamed for him, and for myself. A braver person would have turned the clerk's goodwill to good effect, by passing some veiled remark on his treatment of the last customer. I try to avoid such scenes. There was a train to catch, and was I really the right person to tell him how to behave? This was not intolerance on the scale I had seen in Serbia, but the logic matched. Watching conflict at close quarters had left me with a sombre residue. In the past, I would have dismissed such incidents within seconds, another small drama in the day. But the confrontation at the ticket desk stayed with me for several hours. I had become more aware of the potential for harm, the hints of violence.

In *Civil War*, Hans Magnus Enzensberger warns of the "molecular" civil wars which can break out in modern cities. Economic lore has created "bunkers for the fortunate", "archipelagos of safety" surrounded by lawless zones. Los Angeles was Enzensberger's most obvious model, but one could see similar trends in cities like London and Paris. Now entire countries were going the same way. We were starting to see Europe as a place of bunkers and archipelagos. State boundaries had disappeared; the Balkans had become a bandit's map, a land of fiefdoms and pirate lands. Individuals were unable to resist that change. The result was a kind of moral power cut across Yugoslavia. "When the moral demands made on an individual are consistently out of proportion to his scope for action, he will eventually go on strike and deny all responsibility," wrote Enzensberger.

Most Serbs had gone on strike. They preferred not to know about genocidal killings in Bosnia. Those who had witnessed them, like cameraman Zoran Petrović, had turned away, placing a lens cap over their soul. I had tried to pin responsibility for Srebrenica onto one single person, one specific group. After a month in Serbia, I could see that a climate of consent had been created — in particular by politicians, the media and the Church — in which violent acts became acceptable. Some people resisted; more looked the other way. Yet no one was willing to accept this judgement; no one was ready to accept responsibility. Without that admission, a durable peace would be hard to achieve.

A month after returning from Belgrade, I was sent to Paris to cover the formal signing of the Bosnian peace treaty. There was an element of selfish showmanship about the whole operation. The real deal had been fixed up by the Americans in Dayton, but the Europeans wanted some credit for their faltering efforts over the years. So it was that the Yugoslav leaders bounced from Dayton to London to Paris, like weary athletes on an unwanted and unmerited lap of honour. There was one final obstacle to Balkan peace that day in mid December: a public transport strike which left the Yugoslav leaders mired in gigantic traffic jams in the Place de la Concorde. A bodyguard riding with Croatia's Foreign Minister almost killed a tardy cyclist by shunting him into the furious traffic. Later, the Bosnian Serb Nikola Koljević provoked sudden laughter at the Elysée palace by trying to hitch a sneaky lift. Mr Koljević, a one- time Shakespearean scholar at Sarajevo University, was the sole Bosnian Serb representative allowed in Paris. There was a simple reason for this. He was one of the only members of the Pale leadership not charged with war crimes, and therefore liable for arrest as soon as they left the country. Mr Koljević slunk around in a tweed hat and large spectacles, a Balkan version of Harry Worth. After the signing ceremony, he spied a black limousine in the Elysée courtyard and tried to open the front door. A pity that the cab belonged to President Clinton.

Inside the brocaded halls, the three Balkan Presidents — Izetbegović, Milošević and Tudjman — put their signatures on paper. In theory, the agreement committed all three sides to respect the integrity of Bosnia-Hercegovina, while also accepting it would be divided into two constituent parts: a Serb Republic, and a Bosnian Muslim-Croat Federation. Elections would be held in the autumn of 1996. There was applause and there were doubts. These came over most forcefully in the speeches which followed the signing. Bosnia's President Alija Izetbegović described the treaty as a bitter potion. "My government is taking part in this agreement without enthusiasm," he said, and raised the most fundamental question about the entire treaty. Although Bosnia's unity was recognised in the accord, "will this truly materialise, or just remain a piece of paper?"

Izetbegović's doubts were widely shared. Dayton effectively recognised "ethnic" states, and buried the Yugoslav ideal of mutual co-operation. Beneath the diplomatic platitudes, nationalism had won — and sent a violent message to secessionist groups throughout the world. Many wondered whether the deal would even work in the former Yugoslavia: too many people had been killed, too many taboos had been broken for the peace to last. The states legitimised by war were fundamentally unstable. Serbia and Croatia's political leaders had used conflict to justify their power: they needed more of the same in order to continue. Fresh sacrifices would be needed for the immortal nation, new enemies demanded. Nation states define themselves as much by what they are *not* as by what they are: they enrol enemies in order to reinforce that identity.

In the case of Serbia, defeat had sparked a search for scapegoats — and they had been found among refugees and minority groups. After the "ethnic cleansing" of Bosnia, the next step was "social cleansing" within Serbia proper. I had seen the first stages of that in the treatment of displaced people from Krajina and Serb-held Bosnia. A new distinction was being made between "good" and "bad" Serbs: the search for national "purity" had uncovered a new class of victims. As long as politicians lived by this paranoid view of the world, this dynamic of permanent war would continue.

There was one saving irony to this sad condition, though not one which most Serbs — or their victims — would appreciate. The Dayton accords put pressure on Slobodan Milošević to surrender his Bosnian lieutenants to the War Crimes Tribunal. Radovan Karadžić and General Ratko Mladić were beckoned by The Hague. Naturally, the two men refused to have their day in court (one can imagine their alibis would be rather flimsy). Instead, they chose to stay within the borders of Serb-held Bosnia, with occasional private trips to Belgrade. It was a drab life, lived amid the ruins of a fantasy island. In a way, this seemed an appropriate form of punishment before the War Crimes Tribunal caught up with the two men. Those who created ethnic states were condemned to enjoy them.

And then there was the barrel. I was fascinated by the story of how a Serbian merchant had duped a London fruit trader into buying a barrel of worthless stones. The Londoner had ordered plums for the Victorian breakfast table: his Serbian partner sent a pile of rocks, overlaid with the thinnest veneer of fruit. Both sides had lost out from the failed transaction; a contact had been broken. Like the London trader, I had visited Serbia expecting one kind of product and then been confused by the layers underneath.

According to the article which relayed this story, the original barrel was on display at what was called "The Museum of Trade" in London. Keen for an ironic coda, I scanned the phone directories. There was no listing for a Museum of Trade, or anything remotely like it. I called the British Museum and consulted their Balkan experts. No one had ever heard of "the barrel" or the story wrapped around it. I drew another blank at the Museum of London, and several other specialist institutes. In desperation, I even rang the Department of Trade and Industry Press Office. "Try the British Museum," they said. I hung up and gave up.

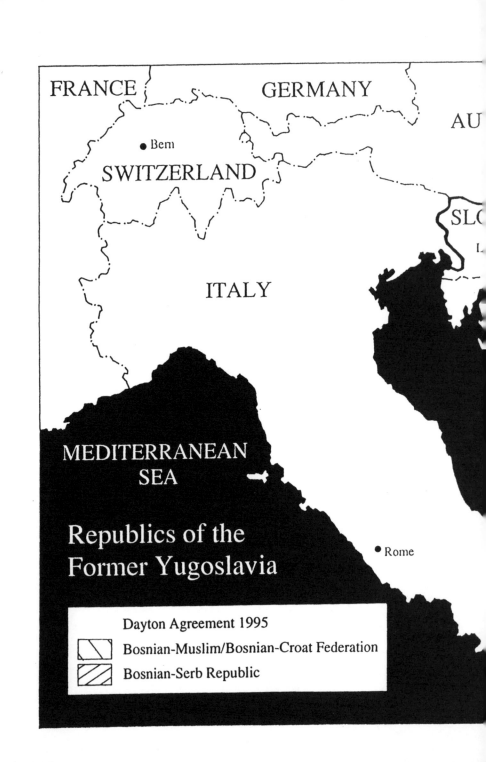

FRANCE

GERMANY

AU

● Bern

SWITZERLAND

SL

L

ITALY

MEDITERRANEAN
SEA

Republics of the
Former Yugoslavia

● Rome

Dayton Agreement 1995
Bosnian-Muslim/Bosnian-Croat Federation
Bosnian-Serb Republic

SERBIA AND YUGOSLAVIA — A RECENT HISTORY

1918-1945

1918	Kingdom of Serbs, Croats and Slovenes proclaimed after end of WWI and dissolution of Austro-Hungarian Empire. Serbs are the majority group, dominating public office.
1921	Serbian Prince Alexander becomes King.
1929	Alexander assumes dictatorial powers in face of political revolt in Croatia and Slovenia. Kingdom is renamed Yugoslavia.
1934	Alexander assassinated by Croatian extremists. New regime under Regent Prince Paul.
1939	Croatia granted internal autonomy. Outbreak of Second World War.
1941	April: German and Italian forces overrun Yugoslavia. Resistance comes from two rival groups : Draža Mihailović's Chetniks operate largely in Serbia and support the exiled Royal family. Tito's Partisans draw support from Bosnia, Croatia, Montenegro and Slovenia, and campaign for a Communist Yugoslavia.
1942-3	Civil war between the two resistance groups. Partisans gain upper hand with help of Allied powers.
1944	King Peter II deposed.

1945-1980

1945	Federal Republic of Yugoslavia declared. Federation of six republics established: Serbia, Montenegro, Croatia, Slovenia, Macedonia and Bosnia-Hercegovina. Tito becomes Prime Minister.
1948	Yugoslavia expelled from Soviet-dominated Cominform.

1950	Self-management introduced to state-owned enterprises.
1953	Communists achieve exclusive political control of country. Tito becomes President.
1961	Non-aligned Movement launched at conference in Belgrade. Tito fosters contacts with Western powers and developing countries.
1971	Collective leadership and rotation of senior personnel introduced to try and calm nationalist movements, especially in Croatia.
1974	New constitution declared. Statute recognises Bosnia's Muslim population as a separate national group and makes Tito Life President of the one-party state.
1980	Death of Tito. Rotating State Presidency installed.

1981-1990

1981	Widespread demonstrations by Albanians in disputed region of Kosovo, a province in southern Serbia. Albanians account for about 90 per cent of the population. State of emergency declared: several deaths and many injuries. Serbs and Montenegrins emigrate.
1982	Further demonstrations: hundreds of Albanian nationalists jailed by Yugoslav authorities.
1986	Serbs from Kosovo protest at Yugoslav government's policy towards the province.
1987	March: Wage freeze provokes massive strikes and street protests. April: Kosovo tension revives as thousands of Serbs and Montenegrins gather in the province to celebrate anniversary of Battle of Kosovo Polje (1389). September: Slobodan Milošević becomes leader of Serbian League of Communists, promising return of Serbs to Kosovo and clampdown on Albanian nationalists.

1988	May: Political and economic reforms proposed for Yugoslavia. Food prices rise sharply; industrial unrest. October: Demonstrations in Vojvodina and Kosovo against Serbian rule. Pro-Milošević rallies staged in response, organised by Belgrade.
1989	February: Powers of autonomous provinces of Kosovo and Vojvodina reduced by Federal Parliament. March: Hunger strikes and riots in Kosovo. At least 25 people die. May: Milošević assumes Presidency of Serbia. September: Increased tension between Slovenia and Serbia after Slovene Parliament announces desire for free, multi-party elections.
1990	January: Extraordinary 14th Congress of League of Communists. April-May: Multi-party elections in Slovenia and Croatia. Former Communists win in Slovenia; Nationalist HDZ party gains control in Croatia. July: Provincial Assembly and Government of Kosovo dissolved by Serbian authorities. Nov-Dec: Multi party elections in four republics heighten differences between governments. Milošević's SPS Party wins 75 per cent of seats in Serbian Assembly.

1991-1996

| 1991 | March: Anti-government demonstrations in Belgrade leave two dead and many injured. Clashes in Serb region of Krajina, Southern Croatia. Serbs there vote to secede from Croatia. June: Slovenia and Croatia declare independence from Yugoslavia. The Yugoslav Army (JNA) — under Serb direction — retaliates by attacking both republics. JNA troops soon leave Slovenia, but battle for Croatia in- |

tensifies. Autumn: Heavy fighting around Osijek, Karlovac and Dubrovnik. Fall of Vukovar. December: Stipe Mesić (a Croat) resigns as Federal President, declaring that Yugoslavia has ceased to exist. Slovenia and Croatia recognised as independent states by Germany and the European Union.

1992　January: Ceasefire in Croatia. Estimated 10,000 people killed in six months' fighting. Serbs retain control of a third of Croatian territory. March: Bosnia-Hercegovina declares independence after referendum. Bosnian Serbs boycott poll. Clashes in Sarajevo and throughout Republic. April: New Federal Republic of Yugoslavia created, consisting of Serbia and Montenegro. Siege of Sarajevo begins, as does "ethnic cleansing" of Muslim population in eastern and northern Bosnia. UN estimates that 400,000 people in the Republic have already lost their homes. May: Sanctions imposed on Serb-led Yugoslavia by the United Nations. August: Bosnian Serb detention centres uncovered at Trnopolje and Omarska. London Conference on the Former Yugoslavia. October: Serbs in Croatia and Bosnia announce wish to create union with Serbia. December: State elections in Serbia. Milošević fights off campaign by Milan Panić. Extreme nationalist Serbian Radical Party become second largest party in state assembly.

1993　April: Sanctions against Serbia reinforced. Massive inflation and unemployment, aggravated by war expenditure. NATO jets start to enforce No-Fly Zone over Bosnia. May: Bosnian Serbs reject Vance-Owen plan for Bosnia, against advice of Milošević. June: Protests in Belgrade. Opposition leader Vuk Drašković and wife arrested and badly beaten by Serbian police. July: UN announces creation of six "safe areas" in Bosnia. Dec: State elections consolidate Milošević's control. Serbian Radical Party marginalised. Inflation in Serbia reaches 2 per cent per minute.

1994	February: Mortar attack in Sarajevo kills 68 people. March: Bosnian/Croat Federation created under Washington Agreement. September: Belgrade announces blockade of Bosnian Serbs. Partial lifting of UN sanctions in return.
1995	March: Yugoslav War Crimes Tribunal opens in The Hague. May: Croatian forces recapture part of Krajina. Bosnian Serbs take more than 400 UN soldiers hostage in retaliation for NATO air raids. July: Bosnian Serbs seize UN Safe Areas of Srebrenica and Žepa. August: Croatian troops recapture rest of Krajina. Estimated 120,000 Serbs flee the region. NATO air raids on Bosnian Serb positions. Croatian and Bosnian troops gain ground from Bosnian Serb troops in Western Bosnia, altering military balance in Republic. November: Dayton Agreement. Bosnia divided into two entities: a Bosnian/Croat Federation with 51 per cent of the territory and a Serb Republic with 49 per cent. December: Bosnia Peace signing, Paris. NATO led Implementation Force (I-FOR) starts to carry out Dayton agreement.
1996	Feb-March: Siege of Sarajevo ends. Serbs leave Sarajevo suburbs of Vogosća and Grbavica in protest at handover to Bosnian authorities. July: Radovan Karadžić steps down as Bosnian Serb leader. September: Multi party elections held in Bosnia. October: Lifting of sanctions against Yugoslavia. Diplomatic relations established between Bosnia and Serbia.

Guide to Sources

Introduction

For a political history of the conflict, see Laura Silber and Allan Little, *The Death of Yugoslavia* (Penguin, 1995). On Bosnia, Noel Malcolm, *Bosnia: A Short History* (Macmillan, 1994). Quotations by Slavenka Drakulić taken from *Balkan Express* (Hutchinson, 1993). References to wartime Germany from Terry Charman, *The German Home Front, 1939-1945* (Barrie and Jenkins, 1989). On the mood of defeated Germany, see Hans Magnus Enzensberger, *Civil War* (Granta, 1994), esp. pp. 80-86. "Draw a circle..." from *War Report*, No. 18, February/March 1993 (Institute for War and Peace Reporting, London).

1. Srebrenica

On definitions of genocide, Norman Cigar, *Genocide in Bosnia* (Texas UP, 1995), pp. 3-10. Jared Diamond, *The Rise and Fall of the Third Chimpanzee* (Vintage, 1991), pp. 251-276.

2. A Serbian Phrase Book

Milošević's rise to power — and the personality cult which followed — is vividly described by Misha Glenny, *The Fall of Yugoslavia* (Penguin, 1992, repr. 1994). See also Jasminka Udovički and James Ridgeway, *Yugoslavia's Ethnic Nightmare* (Lawrence Hill, 1995), esp. chapters 4, 5, and Miloš Vasić, "Slobodan and Arkan's Flying Circus", *War Report*, No. 23, December 1993. On time and "progress", Branislav Dimitrijević, "The Great Train Robbery", *New Moment/Novi Mitovi* 4 (Soros Foundation, Belgrade, 1995).

3. Freedom and Death

Newspaper headlines taken from *Daily News Report*, (V.I.P. Agency, Belgrade). For Čolović's thoughts on Serb nationalism, see *Bordel Ratnika* (Belgrade, 1994) ; "Dead Warriors Society",

"Undertones of War", "Les Mythes Politiques du nationalism ethnique" (unpublished conference papers), "Folklore and Politics — a modern affair", *Peuples Meditérraneans* 61, pp. 165-70.

4. A Man from the Nineteenth Century

Vesna Pesić quoted in *War Report*, No. 14, September 1992. Elie Kedourie's reference to the "indignant eloquence" of German writers is taken from *Nationalism* (Oxford, 1960, repr, 1992), p.46. On the varied graffiti of Bugojno, see Fitzroy Maclean, *Eastern Approaches* (repr. Penguin, 1991) p. 345. Momo Kapor and Zuko Džumhur, *Le Tapis Vert du Monténégro* (Editions L'Age d'Homme, Lausanne, 1994).

5. Turbo Folk, Turbo People

Staub and Kuper quoted in Cigar, op. cit., pp.62-85. Matching lyrics from Croatia and Serbia quoted in Milena Dragićević-Šešić, *Neo Folk Kultura, Publika i Njene Zvezde* (Novi Sad, 1994), p. 231. See also by the same author, "The Authoritarian System: Media and Civic Society in Serbia Today" (Soros Foundation, Belgrade, 1995).

6. A Barrel of Stones

On the story of the barrel, see Katarina Pejović, "A Report from the Horizon of Events", *New Moment/Novi Mitovi* 4 (Soros Foundation, Belgrade, 1995).

7. Milošević — the Early Years

The thoughts of Mira Marković are brought together in *Night and Day* (Belgrade, 1995). For opposition assessments of Slobodan Milošević, see *War Report*, No. 20, June/July 1993.

8. Živorad's Version

On war-related stress among soldiers, see Predrag Kalićanin *et* al., *The Stresses of War* (Institute for Mental Health, Belgrade, 1993) esp. Ch. 3, "Severe Psychic Disorders as Consequences of the

War". Also by the same authors, *The Stresses of War and Sanctions* (Institute for Mental Health, Belgrade, 1994), esp. pp. 133-141. For Drakulić's remarks on soldiers, see *Balkan Express*, p. 89.

9. Tea at the Russian Tsar

Media manipulation in Yugoslavia is covered in detail by Mark Thompson, *Forging War* (Article 19, London, 1994).

10. Stars

My thanks to Goranka Matić and Draško Gagović at *Vreme* for allowing me to look through the magazine's wonderful photographic archive. Borislav Jović's memoirs have been published in Serbia under the title *Poslednji dani SFRJ* (Politika, Belgrade, 1995). A translation is awaited. On the history of Yugoslav rock and roll, see Sabrina Ramet, *Balkan Babel*.

11. A Gap in the Head

For a provocative study of Kosovo's role in Serbian history, see Mark Almond, *Europe's Backyard War* (Heinemann, 1994), ch. 9. Gordana Igrić's phrase "a gap in the head" comes from *The Independent*, 10/10/95. On German war guilt and Karl Jaspers, see Klaus Fischer, *Nazi Germany, A New History* (Constable, 1995). On awareness of The Holocaust, David Bankier, *The Germans and the Final Solution* (Blackwell, 1992), ch. 6. Also Ian Kershaw, "Herr Hitler, Man of the Volk", *The Guardian*, 22/4/95.

12. What Zoran Saw

More reliable accounts of what happened at Srebrenica are provided by *Amnesty International*, "The Missing of Srebrenica" (September 1995) and *Helsinki Watch*, "The Fall of Srebrenica and the failure of UN peacekeeping" (October 1995). See also "Report based on the Debriefing on Srebrenica" (Dutch Ministry of Defence, October 1995). Other reports forthcoming.

13. Tito's Secretary

On the cult of Tito, see Mark Thompson, *A Paper House: The Ending of Yugoslavia* (Radius, 1992). For a more jaundiced view, see the interview with filmmaker Želimir Žilnik on his short movie *Tito — A Second Time Amongst the Serbs*. "Tito returns to tales of woe", *The Guardian*, 22/4/94.

14. Outside the Barrel

On the Paris peace signing see "Sceptical leaders sign precarious peace deal", *The Independent*, 15/12/95.

Learning Resources
Centre